STEM Careers

A student's guide to
opportunities in science,
technology, engineering
and maths

Paul Greer

trotman | t

STEM Careers: A student's guide to opportunities in science, technology, engineering and maths

This first edition published in 2017 by Trotman Education, an imprint of Crimson Publishing Ltd, 19–21c Charles Street, Bath, BA1 1AU.

© Crimson Publishing Ltd, 2017

Author: Paul Greer

British Library Cataloguing in Publication Data
A catalogue record for this book is available from the British Library

ISBN: 978 1 911067 60 3

Typeset by IDSUK (DataConnection) Ltd
Printed and bound in Malta by Gutenberg Press Ltd

Contents

	Acknowledgements	v
1|	What do we mean by 'STEM'?	1
2|	Some examples of well-known STEM careers	7
3|	Some examples of less well-known STEM careers	23
4|	Women in STEM careers	35
5|	Useful skills and personal qualities for STEM	43
6|	STEM jobs at different qualification levels – technician, professional and managerial	53
7|	Preferred or required qualifications for STEM careers	61
8|	Degree apprenticeships and higher apprenticeships in STEM	69
9|	Entry routes for STEM careers – vocational and academic	75
10|	Personal profiles of STEM employees	81
11|	Some major STEM employers	91
12|	Preparation and application for STEM careers	101
13|	STEM information sources	115
	STEM Careers A–Z	123
	Index of advertisers	138

Acknowledgements

The author would like to thank the organisations and individuals who contributed to this book, and in particular Della Oliver, the Commissioning Editor of Trotman, and Jo Bishop, the Head of Careers at City and Islington Sixth Form College, for their valuable comments and suggestions, and Lynne Bailey, who typed the manuscript.

1 | What do we mean by 'STEM'?

Introduction

In education and the media, the acronym 'STEM' is frequently used, but often without saying what it stands for. Before progressing, it therefore seems worth doing just that. STEM is short for science, technology, engineering and maths. The abbreviation is a useful one and will be used throughout this book. In different places, it will show a single subject of study or small cluster of them, an occupational range or a particular job. This will be helpful in reminding you that many jobs are entered through academic routes, and also that most education relates in some measure to working life.

Having explained the term STEM, let's look at each of its four components.

Science

Science is the first and broadest of these, in both an academic and an occupational sense. For most of you at school or college, the word probably triggers thoughts of specific subjects, notably biology, chemistry and physics. Further on, at university, these can fragment into numerous specialisms, such as biometrics, colour chemistry and astrophysics, many of which can split again. This reflects not only the variety and complexity of the world of science, but also the multitude of everyday needs it attempts to meet.

Technology

Technology, the second component, may be concisely defined as the application of science – in short, the means by which it gets things done. This is usually through machinery, often complex in design and tailored to fulfil very specific tasks. On a small scale, a smartphone or iPad shows the sophistication of the technology we can easily carry anywhere. On a larger scale, anyone spending time in hospital, for instance, will be struck by the machines used to facilitate diagnosis and treatment by reading the subtlest changes within the human body.

Engineering

Engineering, the third component, may be described as the nuts and bolts of technology – how it's designed and built from the ground up. Sometimes, as in structural or civil engineering, this definition is almost a literal one – the first step being to dig foundations. By contrast, in chemical engineering, a laboratory and collection of computer screens may form a very different work environment. Engineering is usually first taught on post-16 courses, where its focus is mainly on mechanical, electrical and general principles. As with technology, though, post-18 courses and training can become very specialised, both at university and in the workplace.

Maths

The final part of STEM, maths is also the most abstract. However, it underlies each of the other three to such an extent that they could not exist without it. Computers capable of enormous number-crunching enable mathematically based concepts or applications to be tested more easily before large resources are devoted to systems or production. If your career interests don't lie in such areas, however, maths still offers many opportunities, especially within business and finance.

The value of women in STEM

Science and maths remain compulsory subjects up to and including GCSE level (or equivalent) because they're considered important within education and also by employers. With every year our world becomes more dependent on technology, which in turn relies on large numbers of people competent in STEM subjects. This makes it vital that female students, as well as males, are encouraged to opt for these post-16, and feel comfortable having done so. Even after women became well represented in higher education, biology was the one main science in which they came close to matching their male peers. Recent statistics show increasing numbers of women on maths, physics, chemistry and engineering degree courses, and proving themselves equally capable in related posts on graduation. When the concept of a career break didn't exist, women who stopped working (even to have children) rarely found themselves able to re-enter at a comparable level, or were refused altogether. This is in stark contrast to today, when women are not only well-represented in a wide range of STEM fields, but are normally able to take a break without jeopardising their career prospects. This can be seen even at the initial training stage – for example, female entrants to UK medical schools actually outnumber men. See Chapter 4, pages 35–41, for more on the topic of women in STEM careers.

Pioneer in STEM
Mae C. Jemison (born 1956)

Mae Carol Jemison was the first African-American woman to travel in space. She was born in Alabama, USA, in 1956, but the family moved to Chicago three years later. An early interest in science led her to a place at Stanford University at the young age of 16, from which she graduated in 1977 with a degree in chemical engineering. Despite her obvious ability, she experienced a sexist response from some (male) professors, who, she says, 'would pretend I wasn't there'. She went on to gain a medical degree at Cornell University and spent some time as a GP, as well as providing primary medical care in Cuba, Kenya and Thailand.

Seeing Sally Ride become the first American woman astronaut in 1983, Mae applied to NASA. However, she said her real inspiration had been Nichelle Nichols, who played Lieutenant Uhuru in the original Star Trek TV series. In 1987, Mae was one of the 15 people chosen for astronaut training from 2,000 applicants. Initially she undertook flight support activities at the Kennedy Space Center in Florida, but in September 1992, took her place on the co-operative mission STS-47, between the USA and Japan. She did a number of scientific investigations during the flight, including ones on bone cells, weightlessness and motion sickness. She says that the first thing she saw from space was her home town, Chicago.

Mae Jemison later left NASA in order to set up her own company, which researches, markets and develops science and technology for everyday life. That same year, she was the first real astronaut to play a guest role on Star Trek, the programme which had inspired her. She continues to promote science education and to encourage interest in science among students from minority backgrounds.

Brexit

A recent political event likely to raise the importance of STEM subjects within education, and the careers they lead to, is the vote in 2016 to leave the European Union, commonly referred to as Brexit. Britain's resulting position will mean negotiating agreements with numerous countries, many of them for products and services. Ensuring the country doesn't suffer economically will rely on the high quality of industries such as electronics and telecommunications. Maths, too, will be a vital area of expertise, as complex but realistic calculations will be fundamental to any workable arrangements. These are essentially economic issues, but schools and colleges have a role to play in them. Good ones will ensure that full and reliable careers information is readily accessible. They may even invite speakers from local STEM organisations, and arrange group visits or work experience placements to these places.

Jobs at all levels

The jobs that may first come to mind when you hear a reference to STEM, are ones requiring at least degree-level qualifications and suited only to a select few. While this is the case for some jobs, there are many others where entry is possible to non-graduates, and often to 16-year-olds, holding no more than GCSE (or equivalent) passes. This is particularly true of technician-level jobs, often successfully approached through a workplace-based apprenticeship which includes pay and (normally) day release to college. Engineering is one field in which this is long established, and employees who prove themselves can progress to take degree-level qualifications (or similar) paid for by their employer. This book devotes considerable attention to the different paths STEM courses, training and jobs at all levels may be reached.

The book refers to health-related occupations in both the main text, and the STEM Careers A–Z (see pages 123–137). It's important to emphasise at the outset that these include more than just medicine and dentistry, possibly the jobs you most associate with this field, and view as prestigious. One reflection of this popularity, however, is that the very high entry grades for these which universities can set result in even very able applicants being unsuccessful. So if you are attracted to health-related work, it's worth closely examining all the related ones featured in this book, not to mention the many non-health STEM occupations that you might not have considered before. You may find them equally appealing, and they are often distinctly easier to enter.

The importance of combined subjects

Many students of STEM subjects progress into jobs where their specialism relates to a particular one, and find themselves working with colleagues whose background is in a different one. A basic understanding of what these others do is at least desirable, and may be essential. This is where having studied more than one STEM subject (e.g. biology and chemistry, or physics and maths) can contribute to professional understanding and harmony. It may well be a requirement for specific degree courses, and if you're yet to choose post-16 subjects, it's worth giving it careful consideration.

STEAM

Some recent media reports have featured the term STEAM (rather than STEM) as a concept that in some places has already become a study programme. The added 'A' stands for 'Arts', based on the fact that many outstanding contributors to the history of science, technology, engineering and maths were also strongly creative, showing a talent in areas such as painting or music. Countries such as Japan, Hungary and the Netherlands have students who are among the highest achievers internationally in STEM subjects, and who take a creative subject along-side these. It would be interesting to know whether these countries have had to trim the curriculum in other subjects or make students work much harder.

One large study of employers in the USA cites creativity among the features considered most desirable in job applicants, yet also one of which they find least evidence. Elsewhere, there is a fear of students failing in certain creative fields where technical skill or knowledge is important (such as visual effects) because they don't choose a STEM subject among their options. However, it's likely to be some time before the evidence in favour of STEAM might be strong enough to make its introduction in Britain anything beyond a limited experiment.

 Fascinating fact

The first photographs were taken in 1839 by an Englishman, William Fox-Talbot. In the early days of portrait photography, subjects' heads were (gently) clamped in place, as they had to remain still during the exposure, which then took several minutes.

Conclusion

This book is intended to give you enough information to decide whether a STEM-related career might be right for you and, if so, how to explore the options and put yourself in the best possible position. It offers a wide range of job examples, some well known, some less so. Additional ones are provided in the form of personal profiles, offering extra detail and individuals' insights. It emphasises the ever-improving prospects for women, and their increasing representation within STEM organisations at every level, including senior management. It offers details of the 'household name' employers, illustrating their attractive training packages, which cater to people with different interests and ambitions, and show their readiness to recruit at all levels, not just graduates. It sets out academic and vocational qualifications in full, clarifying whether a particular route is better suited to one career goal, or how high on the ladder you must climb to achieve it. The personal qualities and skills most helpful in gaining or successfully doing a STEM job are featured, to help you recognise your own strengths, and perhaps work on any weak areas. The final chapter offers information sources which you should find helpful.

2 | Some examples of well-known STEM careers

Introduction

A common problem among those just beginning to explore STEM careers is knowing where to start. Of course, you can pick a job at random, but there's no guarantee it'll be representative and the most useful careers to examine first are usually those typical of their field. The essential characteristics of the four divisions of STEM described in Chapter 1 now come into play, as here we'll examine three jobs under each of them. Those featured have been selected because they are well known and they include aspects people often say they find attractive in work generally. However, they've also been chosen because they depict activities and skills involved in many STEM occupations. So even if the jobs in this chapter don't particularly appeal to you, you'll still be better placed to judge others you come across. The information on qualifications at the end of each job description provides a good indication of what you'll need for entry and (possibly) progression. Finally, some concluding points draw attention to how even general features of STEM occupations are not positive or negative in themselves, only as far as *you* see them being. Let's start by examining three science-based jobs, to provide some range and depth, before doing the same for the technology, engineering and maths divisions.

Science

Astronomer

Astronomers explore the nature of the universe by studying the origin, composition and motion of celestial bodies such as stars and planets. Observations, and applications of the principles of physics, plus mathematical calculations, are the chief ways of achieving this. Astronomers focus on phenomena displaying themselves at great distances from earth, like magnetic fields and black holes – most work in a university or observatory, as part of a team.

There are two main kinds of astronomical work – observational and theoretical. The first involves designing and using telescopes on satellites and spacecraft to collect and analyse data in order to test theories, and developing computer software to interpret this. Theoretical work, by contrast, uses complex models to develop ideas about physical processes which occur in space. Fresh observations are compared with established ones to arrive at hypotheses and make predictions.

Astronomers employ specific types of telescope depending on what they're studying. For visual phenomena, optical ones are used, and those deployed to collect light from very distant objects can be anything up to 10 metres across. For examining objects through their heat emanations, however, infrared ones are needed. Observations which can't be made satisfactorily from earth rely on instruments like the Hubble Space Telescope.

Besides undertaking their own research, university-based astronomers normally teach students on first degree (undergraduate) courses, and supervise graduates on specific projects, activities that include delivering lectures and assessing individuals' work. Astronomers spending time in observatories may have to live away from home, as these are usually located far from cities or other light-polluting environments, to guarantee clear skies. Astronomers network with colleagues both nationally and internationally and attend conferences to exchange knowledge and opinions. They also contribute to journals, including well-known ones such as *Nature, Scientific American* and the *International Journal of Astronomy*, and may write books.

Astronomers are very able academically. A good range of GCSE passes (to include English, maths and at least one science) should be followed by three good A levels, ideally two being maths and physics. Would-be astronomers normally then take a first degree in astronomy or astrophysics, though one in engineering or computing could provide a base for an astronomy-oriented postgraduate degree (MSc or PhD). About 20 universities in the UK offer relevant first degree courses, most requiring full-time study. All or part of an undergraduate course may be available abroad, though the number may be reduced if Brexit (see pages 3–4) affects course and project funding.

Marine biologist

Marine biologists study all aspects of life in the sea and the environment on which it depends. Their chief objectives are to improve our understanding of the marine world and to predict changes in ecosystems affected by human and natural disturbances. They spend a large proportion of their working lives close to the coast or on the open sea. Their motivations include a strong belief that future generations should benefit from and enjoy sea and coastal environments that are both healthy and productive.

TV and film have popularised images of marine biologists as wetsuit-clad and swimming through shoals of brightly coloured tropical fish to explore coral reefs. This is a very appealing but rather limited part of what most of them do. In fact, they work in many areas, including policy-making, industry, communications and the media, conservation and recreation (e.g. ecotourism), education and, of course, research.

Those involved in research examine marine systems over every scale, from molecules to whole ecosystems. Often they use marine organisms as 'models' through which to study basic biology as a route to problem-solving. Topics of worldwide concern fall within this field, including climate change, ocean acidification, overfishing, degradation of habitats, and invasive non-native species, to name but a few. Projects typically last between six months and three years and focus on specific processes related to how organisms function and interact, and their environment as a whole.

Marine biologists will usually begin a project by gathering samples and, using computer models or specialist equipment, examine and analyse these to acquire relevant data. The resulting information and conclusions will be published in books and professional journals, and via conferences, many of them international.

Like astronomers, marine biologists in universities teach under-graduates and supervise postgraduates doing research. Outside of higher education, many are employed within laboratories, government agencies or environmental pressure groups, whose work can prove influential in changing national or even international environment policy. Marine biologists need to be physically fit for collecting samples, to be patient in unfavourable conditions or when progress seems slow, to have good IT skills and to be sociable to live harmoniously with others (sometimes for long periods) in close proximity such as on a ship or in a remote research base.

Good GCSEs, followed by A levels, to include biology and (preferably) chemistry, should be topped up with a first degree in marine biology or a closely related subject. A second degree (MSc or PhD) may be required or preferred depending on your interest and/or the level of competition for jobs. A doctorate (PhD) is needed for many research posts.

 Fascinating fact

It's calculated that for every human on the planet, there are several tons of insects. People who study insects professionally are called entomologists.

Industrial chemist

Industrial chemists are very knowledgeable about the chemical structure and properties of materials, and apply this expertise to making various kinds of product. There are two main stages to this – research and the production process itself. Those involved in the first (sometimes called research and development, or 'R and D' for short) work mainly in laboratories. They usually have very specific objectives, like developing new materials which have characteristics vital or desirable in a fresh product. Much of their work is experimental and on a small scale. However, even encouraging results at this stage may prove less than fruitful unless the cost of reproducing them on a larger (industrial) scale is realistic. Chemists who take the production process forward must calculate how the larger quantities of material needed can be manufactured within profit margins. They must then train staff, ensuring safety assessments and precautionary measures are undertaken, and check quality control measures guarantee required standards at every stage of manufacture.

Industrial chemists are employed in the chemical and pharmaceutical industries, food and drink companies, the NHS, government departments, universities, private consultancies and (very successfully) in agriculture. Their work will often bring them into contact with chemical engineers.

Access to professional-level posts is via good GCSEs (to include English, maths and at least one science), followed by A levels including chemistry and preferably at least one other science, progressing to a degree course in chemistry or applied chemistry. Specialised work or advancement may require a postgraduate qualification. It's important to note that someone suffering from a skin condition (such as eczema) or a breathing complaint (such as asthma) may find this job difficult.

Technology

Having looked at three jobs commonly recognised as scientific, let's do the same with three that fit more comfortably in the technology 'box'.

Architect

Architects plan and design buildings and remain involved in their construction until they're finished. Nearly all buildings are occupied, and used for particular purposes, so ahead of making preliminary sketches, architects will undertake or delegate research to ensure needs and preferences are met. The tastes and budgets of the commissioning organisation or individual are important too, so initial discussions can take time. Sketches and plans can then be drawn. These feature exterior and interior dimensions, and perhaps predominant colours. A three-dimensional model is an option if it conveys a better sense of the finished article, or how it fits into the neighbouring landscape or townscape.

Not a brick can be laid, however, until health and safety regulations are met, and planning permission granted. This involves meetings with building control officers and town planners, which may mean more design changes. The architect can then draw up a plan for the building contractor, which maybe includes a timetable for each stage of the process, at which point work can begin.

Architects can work on projects varying enormously in scale, from repairing or re-instating features of an existing structure (like a listed building) to the design of a new housing estate. They usually work within a team, especially for large or complex undertakings. An experienced architect normally acts as project leader, first discussing the work with colleagues who may be unaccustomed to supervising, or be specialists whose skills are suited to the particular contract. The project leader will normally agree tasks to be done, before delegating these as needed, sometimes to architectural technicians.

Architects normally work a five-day week, but pressures (including deadlines) may well require some weekend and/or evening work. They can be employed by local authorities, construction firms, government services or in private practice. Some act as independent consultants.

Becoming an architect typically entails seven years' training in all, split into three parts. Some of this is in paid work, but much is also spent in study, leading to a degree in architecture. Part-time study while in employment is also possible, and scholarships and bursaries are some-times available.

The job requires creativity as well as technical skills, and entry require-ments may vary, some university courses demanding maths and/or a science at A level, others preferring an art or design qualification or aptitude. For employment purposes, the degree course itself must be one approved by the professional body, the Royal Institute of British Architects (RIBA).

Computer systems programmer

Computer systems programmers research, design and write programs suited to controlling the internal workings of mainframe computers (which are used principally by large organisations for bulk data and transaction processing, and industrial and consumer statistics) and computer networks. Sometimes they adapt existing programs to operate better, and sometimes they rely on the specifications provided by a systems analyst. Because their overall aim is to ensure that both hardware and software are speedy and reliable, programmers often install and support programs as well as writing them. This includes monitoring how the computer stores data, sends information, and links with other systems. Security is also a significant feature.

Rather than being replaced, a less efficient program can be 'tweaked' to improve it. What's required is broken down into logical steps which the programmer translates into computer language, which can be very complicated. Debugging is the process of eliminating faults detected while testing or improving a program, which can itself be both challenging and time-consuming.

Much of a programmer's typical day is spent just with computers. However, he/she needs to have colleagues in mind when drawing diagrams or composing notes for the technical writers responsible for user manuals. They may also have discussions with systems analysts or applications programmers about possible strengthening of an existing system, or the need to introduce a new one.

People most readily associate operating systems with computers, but these are needed for all sorts of everyday technology, including mobile phones, tablets and printers, and a programmer could specialise in one of these. Being on call can also be one of a programmer's duties.

The need for Britain to be part of a global economy makes the IT industry a vital one, with good employment prospects for the near future. A degree in computing, computer science or software engineering is the most promising route, normally following from A levels in maths, physics and computing (the ideal combination), with a BTEC level 3 diploma in IT an alternative. Graduates in non-IT subjects may still be admitted for training (mainly through apprenticeships) if they're able to offer evidence of technical ability in IT.

Surveyor

Surveyors are often referred to in a general way, but many work in specialist areas, which we'll talk about soon. Most surveyors undertake assessments of land and/or property. This involves taking measure-ments and, where appropriate, making estimates of value. These can be complex processes, so sophisticated equipment is often used, both on-site and later, to analyse the data collected. Many people use a sur-veyor when buying or selling a house. Typically, he/she makes a close examination of the property being bought or sold, checking problem areas such as structural damage or instability, that drains work properly, and highlighting any hazards (such as old or poorly installed wiring, or even asbestos), which may exist in older buildings. The surveyor then writes a report, which is usually quite short when things are in good order, but may be very detailed when a lot of renovation work is needed.

Surveyors are very health and safety conscious, often wearing a hard hat and other protective gear in certain situations. They need to communicate well both verbally and on paper, to make sure they can successfully share vital information. Their recommendations are seen not only by clients, but by other professionals such as planners, architects, engineers or cartographers (map-makers). They also need a good knowledge of property-related legal requirements.

As mentioned earlier, there are a number of specialisms. Quantity surveyors estimate the costs of building projects, taking account of materials and labour. Insurance surveyors (sometimes called risk assessors) produce detailed technical reports on the potential hazards relating to an insurance application, mainly for residential or work properties. Minerals (or mining) surveyors locate, map and calculate the likely value of mineral deposits. This may lead to the management and development of a mine, and assessing its possible environmental effects, such as air pollution. The recent introduction of 'fracking' is attracting a lot of interest, particularly when it threatens people's living space. Hydrographic (or marine) surveyors examine features of the sea, rivers and other inland waterways, such as canals, often using very advanced equipment. Their reports form the basis of fossil fuel explorations, underwater cable and pipeline laying, and all aspects of navigation.

To become a surveyor, good GSCEs and A levels (normally to include maths and/or science subjects) should be followed by a degree in either surveying or specialist surveying. A first degree in another relevant subject (such as geography or geology) can also provide a platform for a specialist postgraduate qualification. Full membership of one of the professional bodies that represent surveying normally depends on at least two years of satisfactory training and performance in work.

 Pioneer in STEM
Joseph Bazalgette (1819-1891)

In 1849, Joseph Bazalgette began work as assistant surveyor to the Metropolitan Sewers Commission in London. At this time, the city was in the grip of a sanitation crisis, manifested by a recent cholera epidemic. Contributing to this was a random system of drains of different sizes and at varying levels, which made them incompatible. Sewage would build up and periodically infect the water supply.

Bazalgette was keen to solve this problem and, once appointed chief engineer to the Commission, got his chance. His brief was to ascertain the best design 'for the complete interception of the sewage of the Metropolis'. Any plan he devised had not only to be effective, but undertaken so as to cause the least disturbance to the populace of two and a half million.

Using ordnance survey maps, after only six weeks Bazalgette succeeded in drawing up outline plans for southern area drainage, and in six more, plans for northern drainage. This speed reflected the amount of thought he had already devoted to the problem. His huge scheme proposed 1,000 miles of street sewers and 82 miles of intercepting ones, the latter running parallel to the River Thames, and the whole serving the (then) 80 square miles of London.

Despite the scale and ingenuity of the plan, it was not at first adopted. However, the hot summer of 1858 produced such a smell from raw sewage on the Thames that MPs' hands were forced, and approval given. Bazalgette insisted on Portland cement being used in the construction, chiefly because it was unaffected by immersion in water, and of great strength when dried. Today, after more than a century, it still doesn't need replacement.

Though lives were lost as a result of the necessary tunnelling, chiefly through railway accidents and flooding, the vast scheme was successfully completed in 1870. The engines designed to pump sewage over 20 feet at Crossness were, at 240 tons, the largest in the world. Bazalgette's herculean labours were formally recognised four years later, when he received a knighthood from Queen Victoria.

Engineering

This is the third of our STEM categories. It's a very large field, with many branches. Hopefully, the three featured here will convey the essence of most of them.

Aeronautical engineer

Using scientific principles and extensive knowledge of aerodynamics, avionics and mechanical engineering, most aeronautical engineers research, design, construct and maintain aircraft. Although planes are the first thing most people think of in this connection, some aeronautical engineers also work on radars, missiles, satellites and space vehicles.

The research specialism itself divides into two – advanced and applied. The first uses the laws of physics and physical processes to see how the action of flying can be better understood. The second – applied research – employs this knowledge to solve specific problems such as

Want to work in one of the world's most exciting industries? Become a member of the Royal Aeronautical Society and we'll help you reach your potential.

ROYAL AERONAUTICAL SOCIETY

Celebrating 20 years of dedicated careers activities

1997-2017

Who we are

The Royal Aeronautical Society is the world's only professional body dedicated to the entire aerospace community. We exist to further the art, science and engineering of aeronautics by promoting the highest professional standards across all aerospace disciplines.

As a multidisciplinary organisation, the society's membership profile is drawn from a wide range of organisations and fields of expertise, including engineering, design, aircrew and air traffic control, along with professions that serve the aerospace, aviation and space industries, such as law, finance, marketing and recruitment.

What we offer you

We offer free membership to those studying full time or undertaking an apprenticeship and you'll benefit from the following support:

- Free careers advice and guidance

Our dedicated and knowledgeable team will support you in your career development and offer one-to-one advice and guidance such as CV and covering letter writing, job hunting advice.

The Society also organises a recruitment fair where companies across the industry recruit many talented engineers and aviation professionals.

- Become a registered Technician or Engineer

The RAeS is a licensed body of the Engineering Council, accredited to award the professional qualifications of chartered engineer (CEng), incorporated engineer (IEng) and engineering technician (EngTech).

Becoming professionally registered at EngTech, IEng or CEng level demonstrates you have achieved high-level skills and competencies and will be international recognised and rewarded as an aerospace engineer.

- Insight into technical industry issues

AEROSPACE is our member's magazine and each issue contains news and analysis from across all sectors of the industry. As part of your free student membership of the society, you will receive electronic access to the magazine, to download and read wherever you are.

Lalitya Dhavala ARAeS, Engineer, McLaren Electronic Systems

'I love my membership of the RAeS because of the huge number of opportunities I can take to expand on what I know of the aerospace industry, through informative lectures and conferences, organising young members' activities locally, and reading inspiring publications.

Being involved in a reputable professional institution shows that you have the dedication and commitment towards your career and are willing to put in effort into advancing it. I take advantage of networking with a community of aerospace professionals to seek advice and also help other young people to develop."

For more information on how to join and develop your aerospace career, contact our membership team on:
Tel: +44 (0)20 7670 4355
Email: membership@aerosociety.com

curbing excessive noise or reducing air pollution, or to raise safety levels or lower fuel consumption rates.

Designers may work on any scale, from an entire aircraft engine to a single small working part. Computer models play an important role here in the calculation of weight-bearing tolerances and overall loads, critical to an aircraft's successful function. Extensive testing procedures produce data identifying areas needing adaptation.

The construction, or production, stage is next, with quality, safety and efficiency all equally important. Budgets and deadlines still have to be met, though, and engineers must ensure that the technicians working under them are up to speed, without compromising the three priorities mentioned.

Once in service, aircraft still need to be monitored to guarantee performance and safety levels, an ongoing process until the plane reaches the end of its life. Aeronautical engineers work in a number of environments, but these usually differ with the specialism. For instance, much research is done in a controlled one, such as a university laboratory, while production may take place in an industrial or factory setting. Inspection, testing and maintenance, however, may be in an aircraft hangar.

Contracts for larger projects in this industry can take between five and ten years to complete, so its fortunes are hard to predict. However, there are several very large employers, such as airlines, aircraft manufacturers, defence organisations and manufacturers of component parts, as well as the Ministry of Defence.

There are several routes into this work, but high academic ability is needed. Would-be engineers should aim for two to three A levels, including maths and physics (or equivalents, such as a BTEC level 3 diploma in engineering). These should lead on to a degree, ideally in aeronautical engineering, though a number of engineering or technology-related subjects have a place here, too. Employer sponsorship is very well established in engineering generally, and an option definitely worth exploring.

Telecommunications engineer

Telecommunications engineers work on ways to improve existing communications technology, and on developing new products. Their activities focus on mobile phones, satellite and cable systems, data transmission and co-ordinating telephone and computer systems, which help with their processing and tracking. Sometimes they provide a very specific but vital service, such as video conferencing links in hospitals, through which medical specialists can advise colleagues at a distance, to facilitate treatment or even surgical operations.

Some engineers work for organisations with numerous outlets or centres, to ensure the technology at each of them functions properly. When a problem occurs, discussions with business and sales staff may be needed to find a solution, so engineers must be able to express technical matters in everyday language.

Telecommunications engineers work in research and development, production and installation. Their employers include TV cable companies, telephone service providers, radio system providers and communications products manufacturers. This field is one in which the nature of products, methods of provision, and employment opportunities themselves can change very quickly.

Besides the traditional engineering degree route, there are several well-established paths into this field of work, and at more than one level. Bear in mind, though, that some courses or training programmes are suited only to specific areas. However, it's not uncommon for people to enter telecommunications after gaining qualifications and experience in another broad area, such as computer science, physics or maths. Post-16, A levels (including a science such as physics), a BTEC level 3 diploma in electronic engineering, or a good relevant apprenticeship can all lead to excellent careers.

Automobile engineer

Designing and developing a vehicle draws on a wide range of engineering knowledge. Automobile engineers are often employed by (or on behalf of) car manufacturers, but many work on public transport, emergency and armed service vehicles, and even ones designed for sports, where speed and competitive capability are essential.

Engineers whose focus is design must take account of efficiency, safety, appearance and cost. Information on all these, plus feedback from vehicle users, is used when designing or trying to improve a vehicle, and computer-aided design (CAD) technology plays a big part in getting results. Digital-display dashboards and computer-controlled engine systems are also increasingly common in car production.

Engineers specialising in research and development may work on reducing carbon emissions or increasing fuel efficiency, as well as improving the comfort and safety of the driver and passengers. They need patience and persistence to carry out testing procedures until performance levels are met. Some testing takes place outdoors, but most is undertaken in laboratories and workshops.

Those taking an apprenticeship with a motor manufacturer or vehicle parts maker can work towards a level 3 certificate or diploma, usually approved by a professional engineering body, such as the Engineering

Council or the Institute of the Motor Industry. The full-time study route is mainly through a BTEC level 3 diploma in engineering, or A levels (normally including maths and at least one science, with physics being most relevant). Studying for a degree in automotive engineering or a related engineering or technology subject offers better job prospects.

Maths

This is the last of the four STEM areas. However, while each of the other three is dependent on maths, maths can play a central role in occupations separate from the other three, a point which the three jobs chosen for this section will show.

Maths teacher

While maths is on the school curriculum from the age of five, pupils aren't taught by specialist maths teachers until the start of secondary school. Maths is compulsory up to GCSE (or equivalent), so maths teachers are usually in demand. However, relatively few students opt for maths beyond GCSE; of those who do, many choose it for its relevance to their career plans.

Maths teachers follow a syllabus that covers several main areas, the most recognisable being number (or arithmetic), algebra, geometry, probability and statistics. Most of the maths tasks students are set won't be ones they meet in everyday life, but (career plans aside) skills using numbers and formulae can help reduce anxiety and help with money management in adult life.

Maybe because it offers no room for error, or for things being 'half right', maths is still a subject where many students struggle. A maths teacher who is patient and encouraging can therefore enable students to admit to difficulties and help them towards the understanding which makes learning more purposeful and (hopefully) enjoyable.

Like other subject teachers, maths specialists plan and prepare lessons, making or adapting resources. They mark work, and give feedback, especially when pupils are struggling. It's helpful to be good at explaining maths problems in more than one way, to suit the different abilities and learning styles of students.

Besides teaching, maths specialists must deal with behaviour issues, maintain discipline, and be fair and consistent in how they treat everyone. They may also help (and be helped by) teaching assistants, whose classroom role is often to work with particular students.

At key points in the school year, all teachers write reports, sometimes on each student's progress, sometimes on their own methods and success (or otherwise) in teaching the syllabus. This may result in constructive discussions with colleagues leading to a new approach, especially if something isn't working.

Although school hours are fairly short, most teachers work at least some evenings and weekends, sometimes a lot. The majority of maths teachers take a degree in their subject, followed by a teacher training qualification, a Postgraduate Certificate of Education (PGCE), which lasts a year (full-time) or two years (part-time). It's now also possible to train while working in a school, through a route known as the School Direct scheme. All newly qualified teachers (NQTs) must successfully complete a one-year induction period. With experience, maths teachers can be promoted within schools, or go into teacher training, school inspection or educational research.

Accountant

Accountants work for individuals or within organisations. They check that their finances are in good order, and that their money is spent or invested appropriately. Accountants work in three main areas: the public sector (perhaps within a local authority or major service provider such as the NHS), industry and commerce (usually employed by a single organisation), and public practice (where their clientele may be mainly individuals, mainly organisations, or a mixture of both).

Providing an accurate picture of existing finances is one of the most important things accountants do, since (where necessary) it helps their employer to tighten up on expenditures (such as staff, stock or premises), or to see where they can afford to expand. They do this by preparing financial records and statements, checking them for accuracy, and often summarising these in a report which can be understood by non-specialists.

Besides these main areas, there are well-established specialisms. Auditors, for example, are independent accountants who check organisations' financial records to ensure they conform to legislation, and don't mislead potential investors. Insolvency specialists try to rescue companies which have gone bankrupt, while other accountants work in taxation.

Accountancy is an attractive profession because of its higher earnings, and most entrants are graduates. However, A levels (in most subjects) are acceptable as an entry point, as are BTEC level 3 diplomas (though preferably with a financial or business content). Some people train to be an accountant after having first qualified as an accounting technician, training for which is normally open to those holding GCSEs (or equivalent).

At graduate level, any degree subject is acceptable and some employers prefer applicants without accounting knowledge, as they consider them to have fewer preconceptions of the work. Accountancy is represented by several professional bodies, which broadly reflect the different fields of practice. It's important to take the exams of the one which represents the work you do or want to in future.

Statistician

Statisticians collect, analyse and interpret numerical data. This is normally for the use of others, including very large bodies, such as the Civil Service, which employs 1,000 or more in a wide range of departments or units. Local authorities and the pharmaceutical industry are among the other largest recruiters of statisticians.

A full understanding of the organisation, behaviour or phenomenon to be studied is vital to producing statistics offering genuine insights, and not ones designed merely to support a preconception or prejudice. Critical to this is determining exactly what is to be examined, and how to arrive at numbers which, for example, establish whether an existing practice or policy is working or not. How statistics are presented to the general public is important. As this is normally through the media, those producing them are aware of how numbers in headlines can (wilfully or otherwise) misrepresent the truth, and too easily act as an obstacle to change or reform. Even so, statisticians must act neutrally, and have the integrity to present their actual findings rather than what they might have preferred to discover.

Meaningful statistics are rarely isolated figures, but rather ones establishing patterns which may emerge only after a time. This is particularly true where the explanation for something depends on comparing several factors, or kinds of information. Medical research offers instances of this, such as when seeking the cause of a disease, or the likely rate of its spread.

Statisticians contribute to business and industry via market research, helping to pinpoint levels of demand and to best target product direction. In insurance, they enable premiums to be set correctly, and in the financial world establish good or bad credit risks or investments.

A degree course in statistics or applied statistics is a common route into the work, though undergraduates often combine one of these with maths or economics. Competition encourages some to do a postgraduate degree (usually an MSc or PhD) before applying for a first job. Entry to first degree courses may be via a BTEC level 3 diploma, but is more likely after three A levels, including maths. You should only consider being a statistician if you're very able at maths and enthusiastic about it.

Conclusion

Below are some observations about STEM careers that have emerged from this chapter. Each could represent a positive or a negative, depending on you as an individual.

1. Many careers require good entry qualifications and sometimes aptitude in more than one STEM subject.
2. Most occupational areas have several specialisms, some of which entail working in very different environments.
3. Many jobs involve using sophisticated equipment, and (perhaps) keeping it in good working order.
4. Some jobs require frequent travel and even residential periods abroad.
5. Larger or more complex projects often require good liaison between professionals from different fields.
6. Some jobs involve considerable repetitive work, such as in testing procedures.
7. Meeting health and safety standards is often a high priority.
8. Considerable care and concentration are essential to reaching the expected standards of performance.
9. Fitness (and even strength) can be important in some jobs, especially engineering ones.
10. Some evening and/or weekend work or study is needed in many jobs.

3 | Some examples of less well-known STEM careers

Introduction

This chapter now presents 12 further STEM jobs. These have been selected because you're likely to be less familiar with them than those featured in Chapter 2. So Chapter 3 usefully shows a wider choice of careers, but it has several other purposes too. First, it draws your attention to how many STEM opportunities exist within areas you may not have considered. Second, it illustrates more emphatically than in Chapter 2 how many such jobs make strongly practical demands as well as intellectual ones. Third, it makes you aware of how workers' tasks fit in with their colleagues', and their mutual dependence. Fourth, it warns you how few organisations or institutions offer certain specialisms, but shows how entry to these is often possible (or even desirable) after study or work of a more general nature. Finally, this chapter points out that ability in even one STEM subject can still open many doors.

Science

Food quality analyst

Food quality analysts (sometimes called food technicians) assist in developing food products, and test them for safety and quality. This includes scrutinising the raw materials as well as the finished products, plus the packaging and storage methods. Much of this work is laboratory-based, which is also where research and development usually take place. Food quality analysts follow strict procedures to identify any problems which arise at each stage of the production process. Among the most hazardous are salmonella and E. coli, which are micro-organisms that cause food poisoning. The tests needed to ensure safety can be performed very speedily, as analysts employ automated machines that run their checks, linked to computers which record and analyse their results. As well as procedures like heating, chilling and freezing, important features of the food itself, such as taste and colour, are checked for quality and consistency.

When involved in research, analysts may work on improving current food lines as well as developing new ones. This may entail focusing on a single ingredient, such as colouring. On top of their laboratory tasks, analysts will visit the factory to monitor the food at a specific stage of production, when they will wear hats, gloves, white coats and possibly eye-protectors, and even helmets.

The food industry is both vital and very large and the mid- to long-term employment prospects within it are good, with many current workers due to retire in the next decade. Qualifications in food technology are often accessible through an employer, or via an A level or BTEC level 3 diploma in food technology. Further study opportunities include an HNC, foundation degree or full degree in food technology. Diplomas in proficiency in food manufacturing excellence, or in laboratory science, provide additional routes of entry or progression.

Ecologist

Ecologists study the relationships between plants, animals and people, and the environment they inhabit. This may lead to advising on environmental protection, restoring areas which have been spoiled or contaminated, undertaking fieldwork to monitor wildlife, and managing areas set aside for conservation. Often the first step is to identify those habitats most in need of protection, and ecologists greatly assist government in establishing areas such as nature reserves and Sites of Special Scientific Interest (SSSIs). To do this, they may initially carry out a full survey, gathering data to form a picture of the zone, one likely to include animal populations and pollution levels. This lets them identify any endangered species, and establish what clean-up work is needed before certain species can be expected to thrive, or others be re-introduced. Clean-up work may involve draining marshland or tree felling, and care must be taken to ensure none of this has a negative impact on neighbouring areas, such as farms. Besides national government, local government planning authorities and civil engineering companies are aided by ecologists, whose reports often influence their decisions about matters such as road routes. Ecologists also help organisations wanting to establish (or re-establish) industry on a site to meet regulations on water management or use of energy; they may also advise agrichemical companies on the potential effect of pesticides or genetically modified crops.

On established conservation sites, ecologists may work as wardens or countryside managers. As well as guarding these against pollution or even vandalism, they may train staff or volunteers to dig ponds, lay hedges and manage woodland. The growth of ecotourism has raised the profile of access, so ecologists may plan footpath routes, run guided walks, give talks or arrange information displays.

Research provides a vital basis for much ecological work, and takes place mostly in universities and research centres, government departments and private industry, as well as zoos and botanical gardens, and even in charities such as the National Trust and the Royal Society for the Protection of Birds (RSPB). Some ecologists with considerable experience become self-employed consultants.

Ecology is a popular career, with courses and other training opportunities attracting many applicants. Along with an A level in biology, you'll need two more subjects, including at least one from chemistry, geography or environmental studies. These, or an appropriate BTEC level 3 diploma, are the route into an HND, foundation degree or degree in ecology or environmental science. Higher degree study (which may be necessary, especially for research) can be funded through the National Environment Research Council (NERC).

Pioneer in STEM
Joseph Banks (1743-1820)

As a young man, Joseph Banks attended Oxford University, where he studied natural history, the term used then for what we now call science. His main claim to fame is as the botanist (today sometimes called plant scientist) on the ship Endeavour, *captained by the explorer James Cook. This was on a voyage between 1768 and 1771 to Brazil, Tahiti, New Zealand and Australia, a joint venture of the Royal Navy and the Royal Society, for scientific purposes. During the Australian leg of the journey, the ship anchored for several weeks in what was to have been called Stingray Harbour, but which Cook named Botany Bay in honour of the plants Banks gathered there. This was the first major collection of Australian flora, and he was responsible for the introduction of plants such as the eucalyptus and acacia varieties to Europe.*

Banks is, however, less well known than he deserves for his role in the development of the Royal Botanic Gardens at Kew, opened in 1759. He advised King George III on these, and was influential in sending botanists around the world to gather new and exotic species for the Gardens. Today, Kew boasts the largest and most diverse collection of living plants anywhere. A UNESCO World Heritage Site, it employs well over 200 scientists and more than 100 doctoral students and research fellows.

Geologist

Geologists study rocks, minerals, fossils, crystals and sediments to learn about our planet and its resources. This knowledge has many practical applications, including oil and gas exploration, mining, geological surveying and civil engineering. Data are obtained by noting how rocks and other features are distributed, and how the fracturing and folding of these have come about. This helps geologists to age rocks and establish a timeline from their contents, which can include fossils or tiny radioactive elements. These findings let them draw up maps or compile databases for specific work programmes, or for the benefit of geologists in general.

Without the preliminary work which geologists undertake, tunnelling for transport or construction purposes would carry grave risks of flooding or landslips. Some geologists – called vulcanologists – monitor volcanoes to forecast eruptions to help save lives. Others, known as seismologists, study earthquakes with the same objective. Hydrologists find and harness underground water resources, something especially valued in hot countries.

Ground-level observation and physical samples play a big part in what geologists do, but they also use aerial photography and satellite imagery to identify features that would otherwise remain undetected. In addition, they lower small but very sensitive instruments (including cameras) into boreholes and, from the resulting pictures, make computer models of an area or section of strata.

Would-be geologists should aim for a first degree in geology, geoscience or earth science, with a higher degree (MSc or PhD) likely to be required for certain specialisms, or for research in general. School or college students should aim for two to three A levels, including one science subject plus one from maths, geography or geology. A level 3 diploma in BTEC science may also be acceptable. Geologists travel as a matter of course, but some go further than others, like those employed by the British Antarctic Survey, who literally go to (one of) the ends of the earth!

Technology

Below are some less well-known careers which are best described as technology-related.

Orthotist

Orthotists design and fit surgical devices which support a part of a patient's body. Often this is to relieve pain, but it may be to act for muscles which have become atrophied or paralysed. The devices may include spine supports, neck collars, and callipers. The first meeting with a patient would be for the orthotist to assess his/her needs, and formulate the device(s) geared to them leading as full a life as possible. He/she then takes detailed measurements, often supplemented by a plaster cast or digital image, to ensure any device fits snugly. Fitting sessions also let the orthotist show the patient how their device works, and how to wear and remove it. He/she will monitor usage, assessing comfort and effectiveness, and making any necessary adjustments or, in some cases, repairs or renewals. Most orthotists manage their own caseload of clients, but communicate with other medical professionals, most commonly occupational therapists and physiotherapists.

Prosthetists do similar work, designing and fitting artificial arms and legs for patients who have lost one (or more) through accident or surgical amputation. Orthotists and prosthetists work in hospitals and clinics, as well as special rehabilitation centres. Both jobs require a high level of two very different aptitudes – advanced practical skills and considerable empathy with patients.

The only two full-time degree courses in the UK are at the universities of Strathclyde and Salford. A levels in maths plus physics, engineering or another science subject are normally required. Gaining work experience in both an engineering and a caring/medical setting is recommended before applying.

Dental technician

Working with a dentist or doctor, dental technicians make and repair dental appliances. The bulk of their work is concerned with crowns, bridges and dentures, using a wide range of materials, including metal alloys, plastics and ceramics, as well as plaster of Paris, porcelain and gold. Each piece they produce or mend is for a specific individual, so precision is essential, and they are skilled in using both hand and power tools.

There are four specialised areas of the work for qualified technicians. One is orthodontics, which entails making appliances to correct irregularities. This involves changing (though usually only slightly) the position of a patient's teeth, to improve appearance and perhaps avoid or minimise potential long-term problems. Conservation work (sometimes known as crown and bridge technology) involves using ceramics and metal to restore natural teeth with a crown, or make a bridge to fill the spaces formed by the loss of one or more. When the loss of several teeth makes bridging no option, the technician makes a whole or partial denture. This is itself a specialism known as prosthodontics, with a strong emphasis on the cosmetic, as well as the functional, element. The fourth and final specialism, called maxillo-facial work, is the most radical. It involves designing and fabricating appliances which help to restore the mouths and faces of the victims of injuries or burns, or those who have undergone major surgery. The technician works under a maxillo-facial surgeon, and it is very challenging work, as the objective is to significantly improve the patient's appearance, while ensuring he/she retains the capacity to eat and speak.

Dental technicians must be registered with the General Dental Council, which requires the completion of one of several dental technology qualifications available – a BTEC level 3 diploma, a higher education diploma (offered at the University of Leeds), a foundation degree or a full degree.

Theatre sound technician

Theatre sound technicians are responsible for setting up and operating sound equipment for theatrical productions such as plays and musicals. This is quite distinct from what's done in a recording studio and offers no room for errors or re-takes. The sound equipment itself is used to amplify and balance the voices of actors and/or singers, and becomes more complex where musical instruments feature too. Technicians must select the best equipment and most appropriate positions for it, which itself requires considerable expertise, as all theatres differ. Having chosen the items and their locations, technicians then set up microphones and loudspeakers and connect cables to the sound console or mixing desk which they will operate during the performance. For some shows, performers need individual microphones, which the technician will fit, and explain to each of them how to use it. They will also balance the voice of each performer during the show.

Sound effects and background music feature in many productions, and technicians identify, record and edit these. Sound designers are often involved in plays and musicals, but the technicians may fulfil this role, too, resulting in discussions with the producer and director. Technicians are responsible for keeping equipment in good order, and during touring productions may need to set up and dismantle it frequently, perhaps every day. This requires care and expertise to avoid damage, especially between venues. Being on tour can mean being away from home for weeks at a time, during which technicians usually live in a hotel or other temporary accommodation. Most performances are evening ones, but Saturday matinees are not uncommon.

There are a limited number of qualifications, such as HNC, HND, foundation degree or full degree in technical theatre. Some jobs combine study for one of these with on-the-job training – the best source of such information is the Association of British Theatre Technicians. It's possible, however, to gain valuable experience on amateur theatre productions, and you can have a successful career without formal training, but you'll need strong technical skills and a deep interest in the theatre.

Engineering

Here are three further career ideas if you think your future might lie in engineering.

Metallurgist

Metallurgists use their knowledge of metals and alloys in the design, production and safe performance of a wide range of products. Iron, steel, nickel and aluminium are among those they research and develop, and civil engineering and the aeronautical and motor industries are among those to benefit most from this. They work on a very wide range of scales, from buildings, bridges and aeroplanes down to items easily held in the hand. Metallurgists can employ a number of techniques to establish a metal's structures and likely behaviour under different levels or kinds of stress, such as weight or temperature extremity or variation. The force an object is likely to experience in its working life can be created artificially and very speedily, before X-rays are employed to detect any changes in it likely to cause fracture or malfunction. Computer models are also used to make this kind of assessment.

This field has a number of specialisms. Chemical metallurgists study the material make-up of metals and then use this knowledge to extract them from the ore where they're found naturally, or for recycling scrap metal taken from discarded items.

Testing for corrosion is another vital duty, during which they liaise with or supervise technicians who undertake repairs using their reports. Physical metallurgists do much of the stress testing mentioned earlier. They are especially vigilant for weaknesses caused by metal fatigue, the result of stress over time. Process metallurgists are in charge of jobs such as casting, welding and soldering.

Metallurgists often work alongside other scientists and technicians, and even sales and marketing representatives. They're employed in industries such as gas, electricity, oil, nuclear and telecommunications, as well as those mentioned already. The most relevant A levels are maths, physics, chemistry and design and technology (or level 3 diploma equivalents). A subsequent degree in metallurgy or materials science/technology is then the usual path to professional-level work. An HND or a foundation degree in a relevant science or engineering subject could lead to a technician-level post.

Control engineer

Control engineers research, design and manage the equipment that monitors and controls machinery and systems. Mostly this takes the form of electronic and computer technology, like temperature gauges used in jet engines, or gas- or oil-flow regulators in pipelines. Recognising how systems operate is about grasping physical processes and understanding human capacities. Often systems designers train operational staff, and check day-to-day running, sorting out problems where necessary. Modification of control systems is often required, especially where these are dated but need to perform more safely and economically.

Besides working for manufacturers of control equipment, engineers are employed in a number of industries, including aerospace, chemical and biological processing, food and drink, power generation and robotics. Many fairly broad engineering degree courses feature control aspects, or combine control with another major element, such as electronics, electrical, instrumentation or computers.

There are numerous graduate training schemes, leading to the status of Chartered Engineer (CEng). Some specialisms may require an MSc or PhD. An apprenticeship, HND and foundation degree are other options, especially if you're less keen on a long-term study commitment. Post-16, either A levels (ideally maths plus a science or technology subject, like physics) or a BTEC level 3 diploma in engineering provide a sound basis.

Chemical engineer

Chemical engineers know a great deal about the processes that account for changes in the chemical or physical composition of substances. Their work helps convert raw materials into everyday products, such as fibres, plastics, paints, dyes, cleaning agents, and drugs. For certain projects, current knowledge may be sufficient, but for others, achieving their goal may begin with laboratory-based research. Some engineers work for organisations which have their own laboratories, while others are university-based or rely on the findings of colleagues who are. New product design must allow for safety requirements and budget targets, and chemical engineers may belong to teams which include marketing staff and accountants. Safety is not just about the project itself meeting standards, but the manufacturing process, too, and engineers may belong to or lead teams which include plant operators and maintenance staff. They may well liaise with mechanical engineers on the installation of appropriate equipment, and with electrical engineers on the supply of power.

Besides commercial ventures, chemical engineers contribute valuably to environmental protection, by seeking ways to sustain natural resources, and to recycle materials. Increasing numbers of them are involved in combatting the negative effects of climate change. Recent cutbacks in the public sector have reduced some opportunities, but this field is so broad that slimming down in one product area can easily be offset by growth in another.

Before a degree in chemical engineering, A levels in maths, chemistry and another science are ideal, and a BTEC level 3 diploma in science may be acceptable. Larger employers offer scholarships for degree-level study, and sometimes for an MSc or PhD, which may well be needed for certain jobs, and even for a first post in research.

Maths

Finally, let's look at three less well-known careers using maths.

Map-maker

Map-makers are also known as cartographers. They prepare maps and other guides such as charts (for use at sea), models of areas, globes of the earth's surface, and even representations of star systems for astronomical work. To do this, they use existing maps or other documents or statistics, as well as aerial photographs and seismic sensing. Once complete, map-makers incorporate the graphics they've produced into Geographical Information Systems (GIS).

The range of maps is extremely wide, as are the places they appear, and the formats they take, from the printed fold-out ones used by hikers, to an atlas, road map, satellite navigation system, or a version on the internet. Some maps are for specialised professionals, while many are aimed at the lay person. Whether someone resorts to a map may depend on its initial visual impact, so map-makers need a good design sense, as well as a keen eye for detail. It's important to have an interest in geography and surveying, good IT skills and strong mathematical ability.

Map-makers are employed by organisations like the Ordnance Survey, the Hydrographic Office, the Department for Environment, Food and Rural Affairs (DEFRA), and the Forestry Commission. Following A levels (ideally including maths and geography), would-be map-makers can take a specific degree in cartography, mapping science or topographical science. Alternatively, a broader-based degree, in subjects such as geography, could be the foundation for a postgraduate course in their specialism – the British Cartographic Society website says much more about those. Entry at technician level may be possible via HND, foundation degree or employer-based training.

Meteorologist

Meteorologists study the science of weather and climate to make both short and long-term predictions about them. Most of us recognise our local or national TV weather presenters, who offer us a weather picture for the following day or week. They're normally employed by the Met Office, the UK's national weather service. Most of its forecasters work at its headquarters in Exeter or at its operations centre in Aberdeen. The armed services, government and university research institutions, and private weather forecast companies all employ meteorologists, too, and there are opportunities within areas such as the oil industry, agriculture, insurance, shipping and events organisation.

 Fascinating fact

In 1934 on Mount Washington in New Hampshire, USA, the meteorological equipment installed at the summit recorded a wind speed of 231 mph. Higher speeds still, however, have been recorded miles above the earth's surface, in the Jet Stream.

Meteorologists collect and interpret large amounts of data from various sources, and at different times of the day. They look at atmospheric pressure, temperature, humidity, wind and clouds, and they use readings from these to build computer models geared to forecasting. For most of us, forecasts are interesting and informative, but rarely essential. However, in the occupations mentioned above, they're often vital, as accurate forecasts of extreme weather can save lives or property, and there is even a special unit, the National Severe Weather Warning Service, devoted to this. Longer-term forecasts can help companies such as power suppliers and retailers, as hot or cold weather predictions enable them to stock up on products likely to be in demand, from ice cream to woolly jumpers.

Some meteorologists' work is concerned with the very long term, and they establish and use computer models in an effort to see the changes in climate over periods of years, or even decades. An example might be to assess the atmosphere's sensitivity to different levels of greenhouse gas. Information on this scale can be used to influence climate policy at national (and sometimes international) level. These investigations produce not only fresh data or perceptions, but also better equipment for the task. Some specialists are engaged in instrument manufacture and/or testing. Similarly, there are computer experts who devote themselves to the data and imaging side, too.

All meteorologists are graduates, having studied for a specialist degree in this subject, though possibly one combined with oceanography. Alternatively, a first degree in maths, physics or geography can open the option of meteorology as a postgraduate qualification. A levels in these three subjects would also be ideal pre-university. The Met Office offers a few summer placements for college and/or university students, normally with pay. Progression within the profession may depend on study leading to an MSc or PhD.

Actuary

Actuaries apply their mathematical skills to calculate the likelihood of future events. They do this to allow organisations in a number of major areas to estimate risk as precisely as possible. This is essential, for instance, in setting insurance premiums, something people become aware of when first taking out a policy for their car or their home. In fact, there is almost no limit to what can be insured, and how, and fine calculations which take into account many factors are needed. Risks relating to an individual for car insurance will involve data on their occupation and driving record. However, those relating to organisations or property can be much more complex to gauge. This is especially true where the policy relates to potential damage or loss on a large scale, such as through flooding, which can lead to widespread serious consequences.

Health care, pensions and government policy are other areas where the scale of cover, and how far ahead calculations are needed, play a big part. The government even has a separate Actuary's Department involved in assessing the level of National Insurance contributions needed to meet the cost of pensions, health care and other entitlements.

Actuaries need a logical mind, an interest in practical solutions to financial and business problems, good IT skills and strong mathematical ones capable of grasping and applying theories of probability and a sophisticated use of statistics. Most entrants have a first degree or postgraduate qualification needing a high level of numeracy, such as maths, physics, economics, statistics or actuarial science. Three A levels, including maths, are the normal prerequisite for one of these. Full qualification for professional status is through the Institute and Faculty of Actuaries.

Conclusion

Highlighted below are some characteristics of the less well-known STEM occupations.

1. Many of these jobs make considerable practical demands as well as intellectual ones.
2. Major projects often can't begin until professionals in a lesser-known occupation make their assessments or take essential action.

3. Established professionals may contribute to the training of newcomers, especially if this isn't otherwise available locally.
4. A good proportion of entrants to less well-known jobs undertake their specialist course or training after a first degree in a different (though often related) STEM subject.
5. Relevant work experience may be limited, so is best arranged well in advance. Some organisations run summer programmes (with pay) which are very popular.

4 | Women in STEM careers

Introduction

In recent years, a number of research studies have established that many female students, even the most capable ones, never seriously consider the possibility of a STEM career. The main purpose of this chapter is to offer female readers constructive encouragement to enter one. It will try to achieve this by reversing some of the main perceptions causing anxiety, showing that many STEM employers are genuinely keen for women to apply and that, as a young woman, you can do actions which not only boost your knowledge of STEM careers, courses and training, but also give you the confidence. If you're female, then having opened this book in itself suggests you're more open than most to the possibility of a STEM career. Moreover, it's worth emphasising that encouraging women into STEM careers has become a hot topic, with initiatives sprouting within educational and employment circles to attract more female applicants.

In fairness, we need to qualify this a little. First, the entry statistics in life sciences are quite healthy, as biology is a popular subject among female students at A level and beyond, and even the majority of entrants to British medical degree courses are now women. Second, often after gaining maths-related degrees, many women have become well-established professionally in the financial world, including qualifying as accountants, and are able to use their mathematical skills successfully. However, these facts shouldn't disguise that many female students are at least hesitant and frequently reluctant to explore the opportunities within the physical sciences, technology and engineering – in effect, a very wide spectrum of jobs.

Reasons to be positive

Anyone can be put off a particular course of study or employment by a fear of feeling isolated. This would be perfectly understandable, for example, if you thought you'd be the only female in an A level physics class. You might be still more concerned if the course was at an unfamiliar sixth form or college. This could be a challenge you end up having to face. However, if you were to share your concerns at an interview or open day visit, you might find the reply reassuring. It may be, for instance, that the proportion of female students is higher than you'd thought, or the grades obtained by former female students suggest that they've been well taught.

However, if your current school has a sixth form offering STEM subjects which attract you, you'll probably be in a better position to judge things. To begin with, you'll probably already know most of the other students likely to take these courses, and your female peers considering them. Even two young women keen on a course may make others bolder, resulting perhaps in several more opting for it. You'll also have the chance to talk to any female STEM students a year or so ahead. Hopefully their experiences will have been positive enough to reassure you. The fact that they're still doing the course should help!

 Fascinating fact

The concrete which formed the Hoover Dam on the Colorado River, USA, was poured in numerous stages. Had it been done in one go, it was calculated that it would have heated up, and taken 120 years to set.

Initiatives

One of the initiatives mentioned earlier is the Shell Women's Network. This is very active in promoting STEM careers to female students, including helping them find suitable work experience. Another is the Women into Science, Engineering and Technology (WISET) scheme run at Sheffield Hallam University. This too has the goal of getting more women to enter STEM occupations, including helping those with a relevant degree but yet to find their first STEM posts, or others experiencing obstacles to re-entering similar work after a career break. Other major employers and universities are similarly encouraging at a formal level. Well-known companies often arrange for each female graduate entrant to be mentored by one of their well-established female professionals. This helps ensure a sympathetic ear at all times, but also illustrates the organisation's positive attitude towards women.

Work placements

At some point you may want a work placement to see what a STEM career might be like. Your school or college may be able to help, so first speak to your head of year or work experience co-ordinator. He/she may at least write a supportive letter to an employer you'd like to approach, or may even recommend one which has previously offered students good placements. You may have few chances of this kind of experience, so prepare well in order to get the most out of one. After seeing an occupation at first-hand, many young women have been inspired to apply for a university place or apprenticeship which has led them into work they've loved.

Careers interviews

Research has shown that girls who have a careers interview are more knowledgeable about STEM careers and positive about the prospect of entering one. It was once common for all students to have a careers interview automatically in Year 11, but for various reasons this has rarely been the case recently. However, qualified careers advisers still visit schools or are resident in colleges, and an interview can often be arranged by request, with your parent/guardian accompanying you if you wish. If you're thinking about a STEM career, the adviser can ensure you have the correct information about it, and discuss its pros and cons with you. The conversation may end with you feeling determined to pursue this career, but the adviser may also suggest additional STEM jobs to look into. How broad-ranging these are will depend on how good you are at science and maths subjects in general, or whether you're already committed (e.g. have begun a post-16 course).

Contact with universities

University websites provide considerable information about all their courses, often including gender ratios. Most universities are very conscious of these, and the majority of STEM degree courses will show a gender balance which is unlikely to be discouraging. However, if a course which attracts you seems unduly male-weighted, you can contact the relevant department, or bring it up on an open day visit. A course which has low female numbers is likely to be aware of this, and will want to ensure that any female entrant feels genuinely welcome.

Oxford Brookes University

There is a national concern that women are particularly underrepresented in the Science, Technology, Engineering and Mathematics (STEM) professions, with men outnumbering women in most STEM careers.

In the Faculty of Technology, Design and Environment at Oxford Brookes University, we are already demonstrating our commitment to identifying barriers, taking action and making changes to support more women to get to the top of their fields.

Our Faculty has an international reputation for excellence, innovation and ambition and   benefits from some fantastic female role models in management positions. Three of our staff shared their inspirational stories, as well as the struggles they have faced, in pursuing their careers.

Gordana Collier, Principal Lecturer in Mechanical Engineering

Gordana graduated from university in Yugoslavia and worked for the Yugoslav Department of Defence prior to her arrival to the UK. She held senior research and development (R&D) and management roles in UK companies, including the position of Technical Manager for European Operations of a stock exchange-listed Singaporean company until 1999.

Growing up in communist Yugoslavia, Gordana said that her parents, in particular her mother, empowered her to follow her choices, giving unconditional support throughout her studies and raising a family, allowing her to focus on what was necessary to maintain her career at the time: 'We were brought up to believe that women can take up any profession they like – nothing was out of our reach.'

Speaking of classic barriers to women's advancement in engineering – often considered a male-dominated area – Gordana found balancing work demands with family life one of the main challenges: 'I have two children and found it very difficult to return to work each time after maternity leave, but I knew that in order to maintain my career progression, it had to be done.'

Talking of the future and how things could change to help support women, Gordana commented: 'Looking at the practices in Europe and recent developments here, I believe that perceptions are changing and in the years to come career breaks and job sharing in technical and senior roles will become more common.' However, Gordana has found that pressures of a large workload return the time invested when students make contact regarding their job successes and competition wins.

Igea Troiani, Senior Lecturer in the School of Architecture

Igea graduated in Architecture in 1994 from the Royal Melbourne Institute of Technology and has practised Architecture in Australia, Germany and the UK. She began a part-time career in academia in 1996 after becoming a mother and has since worked in Schools of Architecture in Brisbane, Australia and the UK. Igea completed her PhD in 2005, one year after she had her second child.

In her role as chair of the Architectural Humanities Research Association (2009–2012) Igea initiated the internationally award winning journal, Architecture and Culture, of which she is Chief Editor. She has taught at Brookes since 2005.

Echoing Gordana's struggle with finding a healthy work-life balance, Igea noted that women sometimes feel that they have to compromise their family life for their work. Igea's husband – also an architect – has not only shared studio teaching and practice work, but most importantly has shared responsibility for parenting and housework so that she has been able to pursue full-time work.

We asked Igea what improvements can be made for women within this field: 'The primary way that I feel I can make positive change in the work-life balance of working mothers in architectural practice or academia is to write and speak publicly about the issues that need to be dealt with on a daily basis.' Working life should be collaborative and enrich the lives of colleagues, students, families and friends – and not be about competition with an unhealthy focus on self-interest.

Faye Mitchell, Programme Lead for Computing Subjects

Faye graduated from St Andrews and immediately went on to study at Aberdeen. There, while writing up her thesis, she became a teaching assistant, then a teaching fellow. Faye came to Brookes as a lecturer and is now Principal Lecturer and Postgraduate Programme Lead with an additional role as Equal Opportunities and Diversity Co-ordinator.

Speaking of work and potential obstacles faced by women in her discipline, Faye found the lack of female support networks one of the main issues: 'There aren't that many women out there and it is easier often to collaborate with other women than it is to collaborate with men, because their working styles are slightly different. Not all men are macho and aggressive – that would be a stereotype – but they do definitely have different styles of working and an all-female group will work differently to an all-male group.' However, she has found working in academia a privilege where she has been able to have a positive impact on her students' lives.

Talking about work-life balance, Faye relates this to her academic practice: 'In my subject area, we are inherently problem solvers, where we think that we can do anything, we can solve anything. However, that's only up to a point – you need to know when to step back.'

Recognising the challenges of finding a healthy work-life balance, Oxford Brookes has offered support so that more women can reach their career goals. With initiatives such as the Springboard Womens Development Programme, the Athena SWAN Charter and the Aurora Leadership Foundation programme, Oxford Brookes hopes to increase the number of women working in STEM subjects through positive actions, support networks, creating progression routes and providing women with positive role models like Gordana, Igea and Faye who will inspire others to take senior roles in STEM.

Women who've made their mark

Not only are there many more women in STEM occupations than before, but an increasing proportion are in senior posts as university professors or even heading their professional body. Watch STEM-related TV documentaries and the presenters or eminent contributors are as likely to be women as men. The personal profiles section in Chapter 10, pages 81–90, features several women in STEM jobs at different levels, giving an idea of the range possible. Also, see the Pioneer in STEM boxes throughout this book which offer short biographies, half of which are women who've made a major mark in their field, often against considerable odds.

Finally, do yourself justice. If you're good at STEM subjects, or feel enthusiastic about a related career, you shouldn't be denied the chance to progress as far as you want with it. So don't be beaten before you've begun, and remember that everyone is likely to be on your side, too.

Pioneer in STEM

Rosalind Franklin (1920-1958)

Rosalind Franklin was born in London in 1920 into an affluent and influential Jewish family. At the age of 11, she began at St Paul's Girls' School, one of the few single-sex institutions in the capital to teach girls physics and chemistry. She progressed to Cambridge University, where she took natural sciences, graduating in 1941. She started a research fellowship there in the physical chemistry laboratory, but not long after, friction with the head of the lab led her to accept a research position with the British Coal Utilisation Research Association (BCURA).

Her work with BCURA helped to classify coals, and accurately predict their performance in fuels, something established by studying the porosity of coal using helium to determine its density. This was valuable work, especially during World War II, when resources were precious, and also contributed to the PhD she was awarded in 1945. During the war years, Rosalind also did voluntary work as an air raid warden.

She went to Paris in 1947, where she began her postdoctoral fellowship, working on X-ray crystallography, followed by work on X-ray diffraction (images of DNA) at King's College London. This was in 1951, when James Watson and Francis Crick at Cambridge were working to fix the molecular structure of DNA.

The model that Crick and Watson had established was published in April 1953, in the prominent scientific journal Nature. Rosalind was said to have described it as 'very pretty', but been cautious about its validity. Her hesitation reflected the scepticism of most of the scientific community at the time, a view still prevailing when she died (of ovarian cancer) in 1958, at the age of 37.

However, in time the DNA model was accepted, for which Watson, Crick and Maurice Wilkins (also at Cambridge) were awarded the Nobel Prize for Physiology and Medicine in 1962. Watson suggested that Rosalind should have been awarded the Chemistry Prize that same year, but the Nobel Committee does not make awards posthumously. Rosalind's colleague, Aaron King, received the 1982 Chemistry Prize for his work on crystallographic electron microscopy and nucleic acid-protein complexes. This was an area to which Rosalind had introduced him and, had she lived, it's more than possible she would have shared this award with him.

During her lifetime, most of the recognition Rosalind received was for work unrelated to the DNA molecule structure. In recent years, however, her profile has risen greatly, with commemorative plaques, awards, and facilities bearing her name in evidence throughout the scientific world.

Conclusion

The increasing numbers of women establishing themselves in STEM occupations not only at professional level, but in positions of influence, is positive. So are the universities keen to attract female applicants to courses at degree level and beyond, and the recruiters whose support systems reflect a genuine desire to both engage and retain them. These factors have also contributed to making those employers and their staff initially resisting this line to become more accepting. If you're female, all this should encourage you to consider the possibility of a STEM career.

5 | Useful skills and personal qualities for STEM

Introduction

Remember two things: everyone has some personal strengths especially suited to certain jobs or fields of work, and no recruiter can reasonably expect any newcomer to already have the skills they'll need. Skills and personal qualities merge together over the years, making it hard to draw a clear line between them, so it might be more helpful to refer to someone's capacities rather than use two separate terms. Individuals normally think of themselves as having natural inclinations or aptitudes, and often gravitate to work which reflects these. However, being more aware of the main skills and qualities needed in STEM jobs, and how these may be strengthened or combined, may lead to an interest in jobs you haven't considered before. This chapter focuses on a dozen of these. They're not supposed to be comprehensive, but they at least offer a starting point.

Good observation

In STEM occupations, the smooth running of everyday procedures alone depends on workers having good powers of observation. In hospital, a small change in a patient's facial colour or body temperature which goes unnoticed may worsen their condition. The engineer who fails to hear the change in tone within a motor may find it breaking down. The statistician who omits a figure in a calculation may make an inaccurate forecast. Don't think that STEM workers have to be perfect – training, experience and interest all help sharpen observation skills, and where flawlessness is vital, work is double- or triple-checked.

Patience

Perhaps only occasionally a glitch in operations will require workers in some STEM fields to accept slow progress or delayed completion, but in others, particularly science specialisms, patience may be needed from the start. This becomes especially likely when trying to break new ground, which often requires countless experiments or trials. Team projects, where consensus is not always easy to reach, or programmes of work needing the co-operation of different departments, can test this, too. Experienced staff usually keep in reserve tasks they can get on with while waiting for results elsewhere. Some may keep up with recent developments in their field by reading books or research papers.

A systematic approach

A systematic approach is essential to successfully performing most STEM jobs, and good practice stipulates set routines, as they often help in overcoming everyday problems. A set routine makes it harder to miss a vital step in programming a computer or diagnosing a complaint. It also lets staff work faster without mishap when situations demand. When specialist staff or outside professionals are called in, their task is made easier when standard steps have already been taken. In science projects, the exact scope of an investigation must be established in case essential data are missed. Oversights can be calamitous where the information source is far away or access depends on special permission (e.g. to a nature conservation area for endangered species). A systematic approach also helps when trying to introduce improvements, since a set order makes it easier to spot the potential for streamlining or even elimination.

QUESTION

Are you keen to establish an order of steps before tackling a task, or do you prefer to decide each one as you progress?

Readiness to work alone

Many STEM jobs are specialisms, so a desire to work alone can be seen as a positive characteristic. This trait is most observable within science and maths (perhaps because so much work by technologists and engineers in the other STEM areas is collaborative). Once the object and the direction of a scientific or maths-related project have been decided, much of the work (at least initially) can be done by individuals.

IT and related technology make it much easier than before for people to work physically apart, for example at home or in a different workplace from colleagues, especially where team members live in different towns or even countries. They can work together by email, telephone or Skype, showing that working alone needn't mean being lonely.

Solitude may please some STEM workers, prizing the extra freedom it may give them. However, where regular checks or progress reports must be made, fairly set hours may become the norm, even for them. Working alone can encourage self-induced pressure, but those doing this often find that a more relaxed approach makes for better relationships, and still gets the job done.

QUESTION

Do you usually accomplish things well on your own, or tend to become restless or distracted?

Enjoying being part of a team

Accepting (and preferably enjoying) being part of a team is important in STEM work. As we've just seen, people can be linked through technology, but most teams still work under the same roof. This is helpful for regular speedy confirmation or clarification, but also in a crisis.

Belonging to a group boosts your own knowledge and skills, because experienced colleagues can offer useful tips, which you in turn can do for newcomers. In fact, even when you start, your qualifications and level of post may mean you have staff under you. This will mean more than just being friendly, and may include establishing how you think their work should be done. With time, however, experience should allow you to shoulder increasing levels of responsibility, and contribute to a strong team spirit.

> **QUESTIONS**
>
> Do you belong to any teams, or split into teams for some school/college work? Think of why you find this satisfying, and if you don't, why not?

Physical capacity

Of the four STEM categories, maths is the one whose related occupations are least physical. By contrast, most science, technology and engineering ones make some physical demands. Motor-vehicle work, for instance, often uses large-scale equipment in making or refining heavy goods vehicles. Water and mining engineering can involve pumps or cutting equipment being large or perhaps hard to access. In working environments like this, physical mobility, strength and dexterity are often essential.

In science and technology, the scale is usually smaller, but working on handsets, or preparing samples or slides in a laboratory will need care and accuracy. This is notably true in medical jobs, where massage or manipulation may constitute significant treatment, and locating a precise spot on a patient's body is essential, before delivering what can require considerable hand and arm strength. These capacities are also needed by people who work with animals, such as vets or animal nurses.

Dexterity is also vital in environmental science for gathering samples for analysis in agricultural or horticultural research. Marine biologists need this when hunting (often elusive) organisms in or under water, plus sheer stamina to turn over large numbers of rocks to find samples in the numbers they need.

> **QUESTIONS**
>
> Can you think of any job or work task you'd find physically difficult? How might this be overcome?

IT and keyboard skills

For most STEM jobs, the skills you've probably already gained fulfilling school or college assignments will be enough to get you started. Anyone lacking these can quickly pick up the basics through an online introductory program or at a daytime/evening class, but IT training makes up part of most employers' standard induction package. Organisations also normally employ or have access to an IT specialist capable of sorting out day-to-day problems, or helping anyone who's stuck.

However, some STEM jobs undoubtedly demand IT skills well beyond the basic level. This may be to enter quantitative data, perhaps in distinct formats, before any analysis can take place. Findings may themselves have to be presented pictorially, in charts or graphs, using distinctive colours and shapes, so you'd need to be familiar with numerous icons and drop-down boxes. You may have to make presentations to a group, using software such as PowerPoint. In any STEM job, of course, good IT skills mean you can try out various ways of approaching a task or problem to see which seems to work best.

Laptops and tablets now mean that those doing STEM-related work out-of-doors can access and record data from observations made even in remote places or hostile environments. Archaeologists, meteorologists, geologists and plant scientists can do this, but they should have a more in-depth knowledge of the technology, as one day they may have to fix it themselves.

Many STEM workers must regularly produce reports which are coherent and clearly laid out, using correct grammar, spelling and punctuation. Consider whether your current standards of written work are as good as they can be, and work on any you feel might need improvement for a job or further study.

QUESTIONS

Are there any IT skills you'd like (or need) to improve? How might you achieve this?

Communication skills

Because STEM careers are so broad-ranging, particular communication skills may be especially important in specific ones. But here we'll highlight just those most commonly needed.

Communicating via the printed word is not just for recording (as in a report), but also to deliver instructions. Managers need to express these clearly to staff who may have different expertise and/or levels of responsibility. Often, what's written has to be concise, individualised, and speedily produced.

The manner of communication can be as important as its content, especially when spoken. Good communicators cultivate a respectful tone, plus a pace of delivery and everyday language people readily understand, taking time to answer questions when necessary. Most people aren't born with such skills and take some time to acquire them.

In some STEM fields, clear communication is literally vital, as in the health service, where accurate diagnosis depends on the practitioner quickly gaining the patient's trust to ask personal (and often intimate) questions to find out essential information. This is often called 'a good bedside manner', and can be valuable in STEM jobs besides medical ones.

So far we've focused on one-to-one situations, but STEM jobs often mean speaking in groups. Some situations may be significant meetings, where overall strategies or working methods are discussed or determined, and where you feel it's important for your view to be heard. Expressing your opinions in a way others understand and respect improves your chances of being taken seriously and (where possible) preparing or rehearsing what you want to say can make this more likely.

QUESTIONS

When communicating something important, do you prefer to speak, or write? Begin to notice other people's body language; how does it compare to your own?

Organisational ability

STEM workers must be organised to ensure not only that they fulfil their own tasks, but that these dovetail with the efforts of their colleagues and their clients' requirements. Many find a work diary indispensable, where commitments can be 'pencilled in' when tentative, and 'inked in' when confirmed. This also helps them see which to prioritise (e.g. team meetings) and where there's room for change (e.g. to move an appointment). You have to know what others are doing, and respect their needs, by booking shared equipment or workspace in advance.

Fascinating fact

To build their famous straight roads, the Romans used a groma. This is an apparatus consisting of a cross-shaped wooden frame on a stand, with a plumb-line hanging from each arm. By sighting across the vertical plumb-lines, objects could be lined up very accurately. This was therefore a very important tool, and images of gromas can be seen on the tombstones of Roman surveyors.

Performing tasks to order means estimating how long they'll take. Experienced STEM workers can often reduce this to a fine art, but even they can be thrown off schedule. This can occur through equipment malfunction, non-arrival of scheduled deliveries, client delay or colleague absence, or even (more seriously) internal cuts or withdrawal of funding. Well-organised STEM professionals build in a margin to their work calculations which factors in some allowance for the unforeseen. However, sometimes the only way back on track is to work extra hours, though hopefully not too often. Cultures vary within organisations, and some have an expectation to work beyond official hours if needed. Somewhat ironically, the higher you rise on the promotion ladder, the stronger this is.

At lower management levels, planning may be mainly on a daily or weekly cycle, such as ensuring quotas are met or shifts are covered. At middle and higher levels, however, looking ahead months or even years is necessary to ensure things continue to run smoothly. This requires intelligence, a firm grasp of important information, and an ability to set challenging goals without alienating workers. Good planning therefore includes recognising what people realistically can accomplish, and staff appraisal meetings are a vital part of how managers arrive at this.

QUESTIONS

Which of these three are you best at – organising things, organising yourself, or organising others? How do others respond if you try to organise them?

Adaptability

This chapter has shown that many STEM jobs are highly structured and are characterised by well-established routines, offering a reminder that workers must expect the unexpected. They need to be adaptable, too, in dealing with both people and events. Covering for absent colleagues or changing shifts may at times be unavoidable, and a co-operative spirit is a must where an essential public service, such as gas, electricity or water supply, is involved. Sometimes colleague pressure or seniority may oblige you to conform to someone else's idea of how a job should be tackled, but this needn't mean abandoning your views; in fact, agreeing to disagree is accepted by knowledgeable and competent people who respect one another and are keen to find the best way of doing things.

Adaptability will at times mean being creative or inventive, for example when an apparatus must be adjusted to perform a task other than its usual one. Adaptability is especially prized in pressurised circumstances or remote environments, where resources normally available may be in short supply or absent altogether.

QUESTIONS

Think of an occasion when your plans were spoiled. Were you able to save the situation? If not, on reflection could you have done anything differently?

Willingness to wait for rewards

Many interested in STEM careers may have to wait for the rewards these bring, largely because a high proportion require good qualifications that may take several years to achieve. This is especially true in the science field, when those needing a first degree will have to wait until they're 21 or so to earn a salary, while those needing a doctorate won't enter their first job until at least 24. If you feel negative at this prospect, just remember that working lives in the future seem likely to exceed the 40 years which are common now, making qualifying for a career you enjoy all the more important. A compromise is to work for a time after your first degree before committing to an MSc, PhD or a postgraduate diploma (possibly not STEM-related). Although this risks losing the study habit, it also offers more time to consider properly whether (and in what) you want to specialise.

The need to wait for rewards can simply be due to the length of STEM projects, many of which are calculated in months if not years. Science is the most obvious area where this happens, but it can be equally true in engineering, with a big civil construction or aeronautical programme often taking several years.

QUESTIONS

Can you remember an occasion when you found it worth waiting for a reward? Does this usually content you, or do you prefer a quick pay-off?

Sticking with a problem

In many other areas of work, no right answer may exist to challenges – there may only be ones which are more or less effective. Often in STEM work, though, there *is* a right answer, and only it will do. The American inventor Thomas Edison famously tried more than 8,000 filament substances before finding one offering a satisfactory lifespan for an electric bulb. Hopefully you'll never need such dedication, but you're more likely to go far in a STEM career if you're not content with half answers or partial solutions. This brings us full circle to the first three qualities cited in this chapter – good observation, patience and a systematic approach, which shows how skills and personal qualities combine to lead to productive work and satisfied workers.

QUESTIONS

Are you usually content with a partial or makeshift answer to a problem, or do you tend to hold out for the best one? How do you achieve this purposefully?

Conclusion

The 12 aptitudes alone covered in this chapter may have left the impression that your first job will demand a lot of you. This is likely, but the questions asked after each section will hopefully also have highlighted the skills or talents you already have. Discovering how to improve your perceived shortcomings may need a little imagination, but this, combined with practice, should lead to successful results. Ask anyone you know who has a STEM-related job how they adjusted to it, and what they most need to be good at – you'll probably gain some useful tips!

Pioneer in STEM
John Snow (1813-1858)

Cholera was unknown in Britain until 1831, when it struck to terrible effect, with 6,000 dying of it that year in London alone. Various theories emerged regarding its cause, from atmospheric electricity to moral depravity, leaving the real reason unknown, and everyone still vulnerable to future epidemics. Sure enough, in 1843, an even worse one occurred, this time 14,000 lives being claimed in the capital alone.

John Snow was a doctor who had come from Newcastle in 1838, to establish a practice in Soho. From this time, he devoted countless hours to collecting information about cholera in the city and pondering possible reasons for outbreaks. He believed the disease was water-borne and that London's dreadful sanitation system was a factor – this was years before Joseph Bazalgette (see pages 13–14) constructed new sewers. Puzzlingly and remarkably, however, the sewage workers themselves (known as flushermen) were untouched by the disease. This discredited the theory that cholera was spread by smell, but the true answer remained elusive.

Undeterred, Snow persevered with his water-borne theory and during the 1848 epidemic grasped why many of the inhabitants on one side of a particular street had died, while only one person had succumbed on the other: the affected side was served by a well penetrated by sewage, but the other was not. This led to Snow's 1849 publication 'On the Mode of Communication of Cholera', containing not only the explanation, but practical measures ordinary people could take to keep the disease at bay.

Tragically, the authorities persisted in thinking cholera was caused in some other way. It wasn't until the 1860s that Snow's insight was finally recognised, years after his own death, and those of countless others who might otherwise have lived. He is considered one of the fathers of modern epidemiology.

6| STEM jobs at different qualification levels – technician, professional and managerial

Introduction

This is a chapter of two halves. The first outlines the three levels – technician, professional and managerial – of opportunities within the STEM occupational field. The last one is least likely to interest you at the moment, but it's still worth pointing out, as management posts with training are often open to new graduates. These three descriptions are offered here because a vacancy is often advertised under one of these headings, and these can help you understand what each of them means.

The second half of this chapter offers three sample vacancies. The first is geared to someone with GCSE qualifications alone (or slightly more); the second to someone holding (or expecting) A levels or a BTEC diploma at level 3; and the third is for a graduate. Each description is followed by seven questions, which (after consideration or investigation) you should be able to answer to have a chance of success. Of course, it may be that none of these vacancies interests you personally, but they're still worth looking at to get a sense of the range and nature of the preparation you might need.

Here now is a brief description of the three levels mentioned above.

Technician

Technician-level staff normally support the work of fully qualified professionals. They rarely require degree-level qualifications – a few good GCSEs, or one or two years of post-16 study or work-based experience is usually enough for entry to a first post (although for the more popular ones, level 3 will probably be needed). The calibre of technicians in some STEM fields is reflected in the opportunity for those with some experience to gain the higher diploma of the Institute of Science and Technology, and in the Science Council creating the status of Registered Science Technician via membership of a professional body.

Professional

'Professional' is the term normally used to describe people fully qualified to undertake the highest level of tasks within any given occupation. STEM professionals are nearly always graduates, whose degree subjects are closely related to the work they do. If their degrees are not related, they normally hold a postgraduate qualification which is. Sometimes full professional status is awarded only after a period of successful performance in a job, and gives membership of a professional body (such as the Institute of Physics or the Institution of Mechanical Engineers). Gaining a degree or even a PhD is not the end of learning for most professionals. They're expected to keep abreast of developments in their field by reading books and articles and attending conferences. Professional advancement can even depend on having made a contribution to learning, and university staff and researchers are keen to publish articles (usually called papers) in respected academic journals, to secure or improve a good reputation.

 Fascinating fact

The highest shade temperature ever recorded on land was at Furnace Creek, Death Valley, eastern California, in July 1913, where it reached 56.7°C (134°F). The Valley is known geologically as a basin and range configuration. Its base is flat and featureless, several hundred feet below sea level, and much of its received heat is also reflected back.

Managerial

Within small organisations, professionals may largely be their own managers, but in larger ones, a separate level of employees fulfils this function. Often the most effective managers are those who assumed a management role following considerable experience as STEM professionals. For someone keen to work in this area, but lacking technical or scientific qualifications, management (often called administration or just admin) can provide a way in. It may even appeal to someone who holds the right qualifications, but prefers not to use his/her specialist knowledge in a job. We may be inclined (or encouraged) to view managers as more important than technicians or professionals, but this would be a mistake, and good employers value all their staff, and reflect this in respectful treatment of all of them.

Here are the three sample vacancies mentioned in the introduction above. Please read each of them carefully and consider the questions which follow it.

Vacancy 1

Post for a healthcare assistant to work in a private hospital under the supervision of a qualified and experienced nurse. On-the-job training and part-time study will lead to the BTEC level 3 certificate in health and social care.

Activities include helping to dress and undress patients, and assist them to eat, drink and use the toilet. Will learn to take patients' temperatures and pulse rate, dress wounds, take specimens for testing and ensure medical supplies are available and properly stored.

Applicants should be good observers, sympathetic and tactful, but also practical, with good stamina, and not easily upset. Must be a good team member and capable in time of acting independently and with initiative. Good prospects of becoming an assistant practitioner on completion of training, which is likely to take 2 years.

The successful candidate will have GCSE English, maths and a science to grade C minimum, plus (preferably) some paid or voluntary experience in a care or medical setting.

BTEC level 2 award in health and social care an advantage.

Hours 37 per week.

Salary to be arranged (around £15,000).

QUESTIONS

1) Are there any positives or negatives about the post being in a private hospital?
2) What is the on-the-job training likely to consist of?
3) Would you cope with the less appealing features mentioned?
4) What does an assistant practitioner do? Is this a progression you would want to take?
5) Where might you arrange any voluntary experience you currently lack?
6) How far would the advertised salary meet your needs for the foreseeable future?
7) At an interview, what might you want to ask?

Vacancy 2

Post for a Trainee Design Engineer in a large firm which designs and makes parts and equipment for the rail transport industry. On-the-job training and part-time study at college 1 day a week will lead to an NVQ3 and (in time) NVQ4 in engineering design. May develop into HND or full degree study locally.

The work entails being part of a team designing parts for rolling stock. Mainly office-based, but some time to be spent in the production environment.

Qualifications required: GCSE (grade C minimum) in English, maths and a science (preferably physics) and a design-related subject, plus 2 A level passes to include one of maths, physics and design technology. BTEC level 3 diploma in engineering or design also welcomed, as is level 2 apprenticeship in either.

Candidates should have good numeracy and communication skills, be able to work to deadlines, use CAD technology, grasp scientific principles quickly and be able to exercise a creative approach to problem-solving.

Hours 37 per week, Monday to Friday.

Salary in the region of £16,000, rising to £20,000 on completion of training.

QUESTIONS

1) How might your duties fit in with what other team members do?
2) Where is the nearest college to you offering the kind of part-time course mentioned?
3) What kind of mechanisms have to be produced for railway rolling stock?
4) What school/college design projects have you done worth mentioning?
5) Could you explain a scientific principle (of your choice) to show your grasp of it?
6) Have you used CAD technology and, if so, in what circumstances?
7) How does the salary range here compare with other opportunities you've seen?

Vacancy 3

Post for a Horticultural Scientist, to work in an environmental consultancy whose clients are commercial and conservation organisations. Initially will be based in a research unit involved in different projects, but with a view to specialising in due course. Will be responsible for supervising a research technician. An opportunity may arise to study for MSc or PhD in specialism, depending on the company's research needs.

Applicants should have a class 2.i first degree in one of the following: horticulture, botany/plant science, biochemistry, biotechnology, agriculture, or soil science. Experience of research environment (not necessarily paid) would be advantageous.

Important to have strong maths/statistical skills, capacity to plan projects and experiments and ability to produce written reports intelligible to different readerships.

Hours 39 per week, but sometimes more as project deadlines approach.

Salary £23,000 rising to £27,500 after 2 years. Fees for any postgraduate study will be paid by the employer.

QUESTIONS

1) Why might a conservation organisation want a horticultural scientist?
2) Does any STEM area or topic interest you enough to take a higher degree in it?
3) What essentially does each of the listed acceptable first degree subjects involve?
4) Can you describe and explain the purpose of a project or experiment you've done?
5) Do you know of any STEM organisations near you which have a research department?
6) What might be involved in supervising a technician?
7) What sort of individuals or organisations might read a report by a horticultural scientist?

Pioneer in STEM

George Stephenson (1781-1848)

Born into a poor family, George Stephenson was tending steam engines by his early teens at the colliery near Newcastle where his father also worked. Though his parents were illiterate, George was ambitious and, as a 17-year-old, paid out of his meagre earnings to attend evening classes after his hard day's work, soon becoming literate and numerate.

When he was 20, he succeeded in mending a broken engine at one of the local pits and was promoted to engineer. Three years later, he built his first steam engine. However, unlike the static engines he already knew, this was a locomotive, one partly inspired by Puffing Billy, whose speed, though little more than walking pace, seemed remarkable at the time.

In 1819, Stephenson went one better, completing an eight-mile railway track, again for a local colliery. However, from early on he saw the potential of railways not only to serve industry, but for moving passengers. With this in mind, he built the Rocket, which, at an event in 1829, astonished everyone by reaching 36 mph, a speed far beyond anything achieved up to that time. This was ample evidence for the Liverpool and Manchester Railway Company, which had been formed with the intention of linking those cities. Their plan and Stephenson's dream became reality in 1831, with the world's first passenger railway.

Stephenson was always keen to improve the technology and quick to recognise and adopt someone else's idea when it was better than his own. An instance was the wrought iron rails developed by John Birkinshaw in Northumberland, which, unlike Stephenson's cast-iron ones, did not crack.

By 1848, the year of Stephenson's death, Britain's towns and even villages were linked as never before. The railways had a profound influence, opening up travel opportunities for all but the poorest and through the availability of goods and services, transforming people's lives in countless beneficial ways.

Conclusion

The three job levels described – technician, professional and managerial – may have helped you see how far you want (or need) to take your education or training, and perhaps the route you select to it. If you've never looked closely at vacancies before, you can take those featured as fairly typical in length and content. While quite informative, they also show how advertised posts can still leave a lot unsaid. Of course, they need to be brief, but the recruiter may also be looking for the applicant who spots something missing, and asks about it. Don't be afraid to do this; selection is a two-way process – about you liking the employer as well as them liking you – and honest, perceptive questions will certainly make a good impression.

7 | Preferred or required qualifications for STEM careers

Introduction

Qualifications provide concise evidence of specific knowledge to a recognised level. In both education and employment, this makes them very convenient for selecting candidates, or even letting part of the process become automatic. Of course, this risks people lacking these being ineligible despite being capable of doing a particular course or job. However, most recruiters seem to trust the ranks of the qualified to fill their available places. This system may not be perfect, but qualifications can help applicants, too. They offer proof of their knowledge or intelligence, readiness to apply themselves and (having coped with exams) capacity to handle pressure. Impressive grades can promote confidence, too, while modest ones can perhaps lead to more realistic ambitions.

This chapter has two main purposes. One is to briefly describe the main qualifications available through conventional study and typically required or preferred to progress in education, training or work. The second is to highlight factors relating to these which are especially important for any young person making STEM-related career decisions.

GCSEs

GCSE exams are taken at the end of Year 11, covering those studies undertaken during both it and Year 10 (together known as Key Stage 4). Most students take a combination of compulsory subjects (English, maths and science) and optional ones, typically chosen from a wide range. It's not unusual for people to include history or geography, a foreign language (such as French or Spanish) and a creative subject (such as music or design technology) among these. Optional subjects are intended to widen knowledge and provide a grounding useful in broadening options at post-16 level. However, full freedom of choice at this next stage requires at least five GCSE passes at grades 4–9 (old grades A*–C), often to include English and maths. For entry to STEM-related subjects post-16, specific ones (such as chemistry and/or physics and/or biology) may be required, plus a high grade in maths (old grade B or new equivalent). Completing GCSEs represents a major stage, as it offers the first chance for each student to choose a direction in their own lives. Nevertheless, the large majority of opportunities depend on applicants having at least taken GCSEs, and most need them to have got better than just the minimum grades in at least a few subjects. STEM options typically require good GCSE results, though these needn't always be achieved at the first attempt.

Fascinating fact

Some years ago, there was a problem at top-level track and field events, because the best javelin throwers were achieving distances that threatened to endanger people beyond the official throwing area. In answer, experts redesigned the javelin, calculating its weight distribution so that it would fall to ground earlier.

A levels

Most people who opt for A levels start a programme of two, three or four subjects, in the months soon after their GCSEs, and take the exams two years later. The number they take usually reflects their abilities and/or ambitions, and what they progress into is often determined as much by their grades as their subjects, particularly for university entry. Some embark on A levels without having a career direction, and their subject choice may matter little, if at all. However, anyone considering a STEM-related career needs to choose subjects with care, since entry to a high proportion of these requires a post-16 qualification in at least one maths/science subject and usually more. Quite often, a specific combination (e.g. maths with physics or chemistry with biology) is preferred or required. A fairly recent major review of A levels and AS courses (their one-year counterpart) means both are now assessed chiefly by examinations, and the AS grade no longer contributes to the A level result.

Extended Project Qualification (EPQ)

The EPQ is worth considering, and has been popular with teachers and students since being introduced some years ago. It counts as the equivalent to half an A level for progression purposes, and many universities value it for the demands it makes on students to plan, prepare, research, and work independently. Typically a student investigates a topic of their choice, producing a written piece of work of about 5,000 words. Alternatively, creative students can produce a dramatic piece or a musical composition. It is a useful preview of the approach often required in higher education.

BTEC diplomas

The abbreviation BTEC is short for the British Technical Education Council, the body which sets the syllabus, target standards, and methods of assessment of this diploma. These are often known as Diploma level 1 or level 2 (together called BTEC First), or level 3 (often referred to as BTEC National). Each of the first two typically takes one academic year (full-time) with level 3 taking two. Many students completing level 1 or (especially) level 2, progress into employment-based apprenticeships. However, anyone aspiring to a STEM career above the first stage should aim for level 3 (or National), the equivalent of A levels, as this opens up possibilities such as advanced apprenticeships, foundation degrees, HNDs or full degrees.

Foundation degrees

Foundation degrees are shorter than academic (or full) ones and are the equivalent of two years' study, though often initiated by an employer and taken part-time. The study content is linked to the employee's regular tasks and his/her likely future role. A foundation degree can be 'topped up' to a full one, possibly through the same employer and/or institution, though not necessarily either.

HNDs

HND stands for Higher National Diploma, which, like foundation degrees, are often taken at the suggestion and/or with the help of the employer, as a recognised part of training. They're mostly taken part-time and engineering is one STEM area in which they've proved popular.

First degrees - single subject and combined

First (or undergraduate) degrees are offered at universities, of which there are now well over 100 in Britain. Most are studied full-time and last three years. The STEM menu is very long, with would-be students needing to decide whether to apply for a broad-based course offering a useful grounding without being career-specific (examples being physics, chemistry, biology or maths) or one tailored to an intended occupation (such as oceanography, quantity surveying or nutrition). A third option is a joint or combined degree, which divides course time between two subjects (e.g. maths and computer science) and could prove a trump card in a competitive job market.

Sandwich undergraduate degrees

Some first degrees include significant work experience and are called sandwich courses because the placement occurs between two periods of study, and extends the degree to four years. A one-year placement normally occurs in the third of these and is called a 'thick' sandwich, but a 'thin' sandwich of two six-month placements (typically one in the second year, the other in the third) is also widely available. Sandwich courses have earned high praise for offering students insights of the nature of work generally, as well as the employer and occupation. A good impression made during a placement to a STEM organisation will often result in a job offer being taken up a year later on graduation.

The abundance of STEM first degree courses with similar titles can mask frequent and important differences in their content or purpose, so it's important to read prospectuses and departmental websites carefully. Whatever their format, first degrees in STEM subjects normally lead to the award of Bachelor of Science, which is shortened to BSc.

Higher degrees

Admission to a higher degree in a STEM subject normally requires a first degree in the same subject, or a closely related one. Most come at one of two levels, known as master's (MSc) or doctorate (PhD or DPhil). Successful full-time study usually leads to the former being awarded after one academic year, while the latter takes three. Some MSc and PhD programmes are offered part-time, but normally take twice as long. Others, however, can only be undertaken full-time because constant access to a laboratory, or specialised equipment, is necessary.

At master's level, it's often possible to choose between study which follows a syllabus (often called a 'taught' course) and doing a research project. In contrast, doctorates are nearly always by research. The attractions of a higher degree may only become evident some way into a first degree, when career decisions become more urgent. However, there are STEM fields (and science ones in particular) where reaching full professional level is almost certain to require a doctorate.

UNIVERSITY *of York*
Department of Physics

Studying Physics

Physics is fundamental to our understanding of how the universe works. By choosing to take a degree in physics, you choose to study an enormously stimulating subject that also sits right at the heart of technology development. Physics today is a very rewarding and exciting field with new discoveries occurring at the frontiers of human knowledge. Its methods and insights are widely applicable and its practitioners widely sought.

Physics at York

Our flexible programmes allow students to maintain a wide-ranging approach to physics or to specialise in a particular area. Students are able to further tailor their course to their interests by studying abroad or by conducting a research placement. All our programmes are accredited by the Institute of Physics (IOP) and are structured around core teaching which ensures that students have a solid grounding in the key concepts of physics.

We offer an integrated Year Abroad programme alongside all of our Physics programs. Studying or working abroad during your degree is a life-changing experience that can boost your self-confidence, independence and ambition. It also broadens your cultural and social perspectives, develops language skills and significantly increases your employability in the global jobs market.

The White Rose Industrial Physics Academy (WRIPA), a new collaboration between the Universities of York and Sheffield and technical industry partners aims to improve the industry-relevant skills of physics graduates. The Academy is setting up industry-led undergraduate projects, enhancing the industry focus of the taught curriculum and organising joint workshops and recruitment events to enhance the industry skills of our graduates.

You will be taught by world leading academics at the cutting edge of their research field who possess an enthusiasm for teaching. This fosters excellent staff-student rapport and ensures an extremely friendly and supportive atmosphere. Regular supervisions meetings, small group tutorials and our 'open door' policy for approaching our academic staff are distinctive in our teaching approach and enable students to share their insights and develop a deeper understanding of their subject.

Our department is rapidly expanding with world leading research programmes in several areas of physics including Condensed Matter Physics, Nuclear Physics, Plasma Physics, Quantum Computing, Nanophysics, Nuclear Astrophysics and Fusion. There has recently been significant major investment in our laboratories and facilities including our new Quantum Technology Hub, York-JEOL Nanocentre, York Plasma Institute and our Astrocampus.

You will have excellent career prospects with 87% of graduates in employment or further study after six months after graduating. We pride ourselves on being a friendly and supportive department, helping students to unlock their academic potential and develop skills that are highly sought after by employers. We hold a Juno Champion Award for support of women in physics and have achieved a Silver Athena SWAN accreditation for our ongoing support of women in science.

For further information on studying at York:
www.york.ac.uk/physics
+44 (0)1904 322241
physics-admissions@york.ac.uk

Pioneer in STEM
Jane C. Wright (1919-2013)

Born in New York in 1919, Jane C Wright earned a degree in art from Smith College in 1942. She then began medical training, her father having been one of the first Afro-Americans to graduate in medicine from Harvard. She qualified and later joined her father doing research at Harlem Hospital Cancer Research Center. In due course she became Director of Cancer Research at New York University.

When she began researching, testing the potential effects of anti-cancer drugs was done on laboratory mice. However, Jane established testing on tissue culture as a more effective approach. She was also the first person to identify methotrexate as a foundation chemotherapy drug, mainly in the treatment of breast and skin cancer. Over the years, this saved millions of lives, as it became common practice in relation to cancer treatment generally.

Jane Wright's later research was in developing chemotherapeutics. Her contribution here (again, breaking with common practice) was to introduce variations in drug dosages and change the delivery sequence of different drugs, which increased effectiveness and minimised side effects. Her chemotherapy protocols extended the lifespan of skin cancer patients by up to 10 years.

During her career, Jane Wright published well over 70 papers on cancer chemotherapy. In 1964, she was one of the seven founders of the American Society of Clinical Oncology, and in 1971 she became the first woman president of the New York Cancer Society. She was also active internationally, leading delegations to China, the Soviet Union, Ghana and Kenya. Through her career, she overcame the prejudices against her both as a woman and as a black person, and made a great contribution in her field. She died only a few years ago, at the age of 93.

Intermediate and advanced apprenticeships

Intermediate and advanced apprenticeships lead to a national, recognised qualification, such as a HND or BTEC. They are available in a wide range of STEM occupational areas, especially technology and engineering. Most commit you to five days a week, normally four in the workplace, for on-the-job training and experience, and one at a local college or the employer's training centre. Apprentices are paid, their allowance normally rising with each year, or on reaching their

LearnChemistry

Our free resource website

Videos, games, tutorials, podcasts and more
– to help you learn, revise and discover
chemistry

Like puzzles?

Search for 'gridlocks' and learn the chemis
facts you need for your exams.

Plus, check out the interactive version of th
periodic table online, or download the app.
mixes element data with loads of interesting
facts – including history, alchemy and scarci
– and links to podcasts and videos.

rsc.li/learn-chemistry

A **Future** in Chemistry

Discover your future in chemistry with our
careers website

Learn more about your career and study options in
chemistry.

Decide between university and vocational routes.

Choose your career path by picking
the right course and exploring
real-life job profiles.

rsc.li/future-in-chemistry

ROYAL SOCIETY
OF **CHEMISTRY**

Registered charity number: 207890

Tomorrow's Engineers

Are you a creative problem-solver?

Engineers are creative thinkers that design, create and innovate to improve lives.

Engineering is behind everything – from smartphones and hair styling products to prosthetic limbs and wind farms.

Read hundreds of real stories on the Tomorrow's Engineers website.

tomorrowsengineers.org.uk/real-jobs

Whatever you're into – whether it's food or sport, space or the environment, there's a world of exciting opportunities in engineering. You could travel the globe, meet interesting people and even save lives.

Real job:

Jaz Rabadia MBE, Senior Manager of Energy & Initiatives at Starbucks

❞ Engineering is not about what you do, but how you think ❞

NEW!

Tomorrow's Engineers
From idea to career
Explore 12 areas of engineering

Find out more about the different types of engineering and where they could take you, here:

tomorrowsengineers.org.uk/from-idea-to-career

Department of Physics

Highest quality physics education in a leading research environment. Our enthusiasm for teaching and excellent staff-student rapport ensure an extremely supportive atmosphere.

- Our lectures, laboratories and small group teaching are designed to increase your future employability
- Student-led research projects in Nano Physics, Plasma, Nuclear and Astrophysics
- Industrial placements and study abroad options available
- Our courses are accredited by the Institute of Physics (IOP) and are offered as integrated masters or bachelors degrees
- Different strands available including Physics with Astrophysics, Theoretical Physics, Physics with Philosophy, Physics and Mathematics or Physics as a single subject

Please visit **www.york.ac.uk/physics** for more information

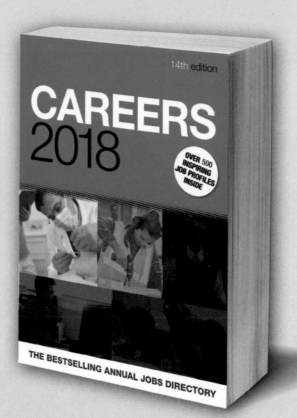

qualification goal. No employer is obliged to keep someone on beyond this point, but most will want to, at which point they gain full employee status. Whether progression to a higher or degree apprenticeship (see below) is possible will depend on the employer and perhaps the nature of the business.

It's very important to recognise that progression from school or college into an apprenticeship of any kind or at any level is not guaranteed. Some GCSE qualifications are likely to be required, but many factors are taken into account when assessing an applicant's suitability. Apprenticeships with household-name organisations, or even local ones with a good reputation, can attract very good candidates, resulting in strong competition.

Higher and degree apprenticeships

Higher and degree apprenticeships were introduced to Britain only recently, but in that short time have proved popular even with well-known organisations. Those running them typically advertise for applicants holding (or expecting to gain) A levels or their BTEC equivalent, with a view to offering successful ones on-the-job training combined with formal study to reach NVQ4 and above, or a degree. See Chapter 8, pages 69–74, for more information.

A year out

On completing a qualification, especially after A levels or a first degree, many students take a year out, also known as a gap year, to think about their situation and career prospects. This is often a good move, especially if you take a job that offers a taste of work which might appeal in the long term. It also offers an excellent chance to do something significant or adventurous before a career or further study makes this difficult. You may want to tour different countries, or do work which may be modestly paid but provides a taste of an unfamiliar and interesting culture. There are organisations which have numerous fascinating programmes and can help you arrange one. See also www.gap-year.com.

Conclusion

At certain points, opting for a particular qualification will hinge on whether you want to be a generalist or a specialist. Each has its pros and cons. A generalist can keep his/her 'hand in' on a variety of skills, for instance, by spending workplace time in different departments, or by changing employer every so often. This offers interest and more chance of adapting to circumstances in the event of a slump or redundancies. A specialist, by contrast, will have a specific skill, perhaps cultivated to a high level. This may result in greater job satisfaction, but makes it harder to ride any winds of change and, though specialists sometimes enjoy more prestige than generalists, they can be more vulnerable. However, the preference to be one or the other is something you may discover only after some years in employment.

8 | Degree apprenticeships and higher apprenticeships in STEM

Introduction

The purpose of this chapter is to introduce higher and degree apprenticeships. This is important because they were only introduced a few years ago, meaning that some people won't even have heard of them, while many who have may still be unclear as to whether or how they differ. At the time of writing, degree apprenticeships in Britain were expected soon to hit the 5,000 mark, with higher apprenticeships also growing strongly in popularity. Both programmes operate separately from the university application system (UCAS) and there's nothing to stop someone attracted by these work-based routes from applying simultaneously for a conventional full-time degree course. In fact, unless you have an aversion to full-time higher education, this may be a sensible plan.

 Fascinating fact

British RAF pilot Andy Green set the world land speed record of 763 mph at Black Rock Desert, Nevada, USA. The car, *Thrust SSC*, was jet-propelled and broke the sound barrier on land exactly 50 years after it was first broken in a plane. The desert is composed of lava beds and alkali flats, providing an even surface for many miles, as it was once a lake bed.

Degree apprenticeships

Launched in September 2015, degree apprenticeships are the most recent major initiative to encourage work-based learning. They offer the chance to gain a full bachelor's degree or even master's degree alongside the benefits of fieldwork and training. Each programme is the product of a partnership between a university and an employer, and can take from three to six years to complete, depending on the level, or the circumstances in which the programme takes place. Normally the professional body an employer is affiliated to is also involved, to ensure that the standards of learning and performance are suitable to award professional status at the end.

A degree apprenticeship can be understood in one of two ways.

1. As an individually designed package drawn up by the employer, university and professional body.
2. By the employer plugging into an existing university degree programme already recognised as appropriate, the work-based part being determined by the employer, with professional body approval.

The apprentices have employee status throughout. Their study may be undertaken on a regular (probably weekly) day-release or occasional block-release basis, by arrangement. Programmes are constructed around existing models of sandwich degrees, where students typically spend a year in industry. It's expected that the quality of the new programmes will encourage even higher retention rates than usual, with the current figure standing at over 80%. This is likely to rise as, where a new degree is proposed, employers will be able to negotiate with the university to maximise its suitability and appeal.

For degree apprentices, each programme offers the following major benefits:

*   a respectable level of pay throughout
*   a bachelor's or master's degree
*   no university fees to pay
*   recognition by the appropriate professional body
*   a responsible job role or promotion on completion.

The employer also gains by being more likely to attract high-calibre school/college leavers otherwise destined for university, and because the government contributes to the cost of training.

Degree apprentices are assessed at the end of the programme, both in their academic learning and occupational competence. Competition for places is always likely to be strong, since current employees are also eligible. Growth in degree apprenticeships could be rapid, as the quality and career progress of those completing them become increasingly evident. Anyone interested should do some research and allow plenty of time to prepare a well-considered application. Many of those degree apprenticeships already established are in STEM areas.

Examples of opportunities available

Teesside University is one institution with an impressive range of degree (and higher) apprenticeships. Three it offers in the first category are digital technology (web engineering), embedded electronics systems design and laboratory science. One of the employers it's linked to is BAM Nuttall Ltd, a construction and civil engineering company with headquarters in Canterbury, but bases elsewhere in the UK too.

The University of Manchester's Faculty of Science and Engineering offers a degree apprenticeship programme, while Aston University has one in digital and technology solutions. Aston's website features an apprentice who worked on projects in five cities.

Higher apprenticeships

Higher apprenticeships offer most of the features and benefits of their degree counterparts. However, they offer training initially for NVQ levels 4 and 5 (equivalent to a higher education certificate or diploma, or a foundation degree), with progression to levels 6 and 7 (to bachelor's or master's) often possible but not automatic. Nevertheless, a higher apprenticeship below degree level can still contribute to the admissions requirements of a university for a degree course, and/or to a professional qualification from an industrial governing body in the UK.

Two examples of recently advertised higher apprenticeships will provide an idea of the sort of jobs for which they can offer training.

Higher apprenticeships in IT, software, web and telecommunications

Roles include:

IT project manager: overseeing the development of computer systems to meet clients' needs.

Analyst developer: to research, design and write new software programs.

Security analyst: to assess risks to systems, design and develop security plans.

Entry requirements: two A levels or an advanced apprenticeship in ICT. This leads to a level 4 qualification.

Average salary: £200/week.

> ## Higher apprenticeship for life sciences and chemical science professionals
>
> Roles include:
>
> **Product analyst**
>
> **Colourist**
>
> **Quality control technician**
>
> **Laboratory technician**
>
> **Veterinary pathologist.**
>
> Well suited to industries such as pharmaceuticals, petro-chemicals, marine science, mining and quarrying, environmental science, the nuclear industry, and research and development and scientific analysis generally.
>
> **Entry requirements:** two A levels (including a science subject), BTEC level 3 in science, or relevant advanced apprenticeship.

A good general website for degree and higher apprenticeships is www.gov.uk/government/publications/higher-and-degree-apprenticeships.

> ### Pioneer in STEM
> ### *Jocelyn Bell Burnell (born 1943)*
>
> *Susan Jocelyn Bell was born in County Armagh, Northern Ireland, where her father was an architect. He had helped design the Armagh Planetarium, something which from an early age prompted her interest in astronomy. However, the local school she attended had a policy of not allowing girls to study science, but in time abandoned this owing to protests, many of them from parents.*
>
> *Jocelyn failed her 11+ exam, but went to a Quaker secondary school in York, where she was inspired by her physics teacher. He impressed on her that the subject was more about applying a few key principles than memorising a lot of facts. In due course, she graduated from the University of Glasgow in 1965 with a BSc in physics and shortly afterwards enrolled at Cambridge to do post-graduate study in astrophysics.*

In 1967, she was the first person to observe radio pulsars (pulsating stars). Pulsars emit beams of electromagnetic radiation at very precise intervals, which makes them very useful time-keepers, and the first planets beyond our solar system were discovered around a pulsar.

The significance of the discovery was reflected in the award of the 1974 Nobel Prize for Physics, which included Jocelyn's doctoral supervisor, but not her. This was controversial, the Nobel Committee itself being openly criticised by some eminent figures. However, Bell herself said that the Prize might be devalued if awarded to a research student, except in very exceptional cases, of which she did not consider herself one.

Now Dame Jocelyn Bell Burnell, she has received countless awards and distinctions, including President of the Royal Astronomical Society, President of the Institute of Physics and Visiting Professor at Oxford University. She has also for many years campaigned to improve the status and raise the number of women within the physics and astronomy communities worldwide.

Some possible negatives

Perhaps the positive elements in this picture of degree and higher apprenticeships make other options pale by comparison. It's true that for money and practical experience the apprenticeship route may seem hard to beat, but bear in mind that not going to university (for instance) may mean missing out on some worthwhile attractions. One is the long summer holidays which offer scope for travel, work or voluntary activities unrelated to your career plans. Similarly, the workplace is unlikely to offer the chance to pursue a sport or cultural activity like music or drama at the standard or for the time which the campus would, or to mix with people interested or engaged in activities quite different from your own.

And afterwards ...?

An organisation which invests the resources needed to put you through a degree or higher apprenticeship programme will almost certainly want you, on completion, to stay with them for a while, a salary increase and/or promotion being likely incentives. However, there may also be an obligation – moral if not legal – to remain for a minimum period, so (even before applying) ensure you know where you'd stand in this respect if you wanted to move on. The positive comments and evident enthusiasm about the prospects of the apprentices featured on many company websites, however, may make you feel you're more than likely to want to stay. See Chapter 13, pages 115–121, for sources of additional information.

Conclusion

The opportunity to get a degree free of debt and learn valuable job skills and occupational knowledge make the degree or higher apprenticeship package a very appealing option. However, remember that if you're drawn to it, many others will be attracted, too, and selection may be just as competitive as higher education. Missing the non-academic side of university life may or may not matter to you, but consider too that an apprenticeship may cater less for altered preference than higher education, which can, for instance, often allow for interest in a specialism that many students experience only part way through their first degree.

This places the onus firmly on any would-be applicant to investigate fully not only the apprenticeship, but the extent of options on completion, bearing in mind that for a time these will almost certainly be confined to the recruiting organisation.

9 | Entry routes for STEM careers - vocational and academic

Introduction

The purpose of this chapter is to lay out the paths you can take towards a STEM-related career after GCSEs, the first point at which real choice is possible. It will highlight the advantages and possible hazards of each of the main routes and emphasise where higher and degree apprentice ships constitute a significant broadening of options.

When people talk about career direction, they often refer to the academic route or the vocational one, so it seems worthwhile explaining what these terms mean. Each term implies a definite direction, with its stages together forming a straight line. This sounds reasonable, as the academic route after GCSEs is usually taken to mean A levels, followed by a first degree studied full-time and possibly followed by a higher one. This is different from the vocational route, which is based in or leading towards an occupational area, or even a specific job.

The vocational route, however, can take one of two forms. After GCSEs, the first may be called the 'study' option, consisting of a BTEC level 2 or level 3 diploma, then work-based training and part-time study for a qualification such as NVQ4 and above. The second form we'll call the 'training' option, where there's no preliminary vocational study and both experience and study are through employer-based formats (usually an apprenticeship) from the start.

Let's now look at the main entry routes. None is put forward as being the right or the best one, because none of them is. Rather it's a matter of judging which is most likely to be appropriate for you. Everyone is different and it's essential that the choice (whenever you make it) reflects your own wishes and knowledge of yourself.

Why take A levels?

A levels represent the traditional way into jobs in the maths division of STEM, and the pure science one, which covers fields such as chemistry, biology and physics. A subject selection of at least two of these plus maths will leave you a very wide range of STEM study and work-based options at the next stage. If you have a specific career in mind, two alone will be fine, but these must be the most relevant (e.g. chemistry and biology for most medicine-related ones). Occasionally, a subject outside these will be useful, but probably where a slightly unusual career is the goal and fairly obvious (e.g. A level Geology for a would-be geologist).

Compared with GCSEs, you'll spend a lot of time on each A level subject, so try to avoid any you're not keen on. Also, just passing may not be enough; intending doctors need excellent grades, as do would-be dentists and pharmacists, and more modest (but still good) ones are expected for degree courses such as nutrition, physiotherapy, radiography and laboratory sciences. A levels will keep most STEM options open the longest.

Why take a BTEC diploma?

A BTEC level 2 diploma (for example, in engineering) is an adequate platform for someone keen to do work-based training, but preferring a proper taster of this first through a one-year college/sixth-form course. This often proves worthwhile – many people at 16 aren't quite ready for a work environment and this offers time to mature, frequently including an employer placement. A level 3 diploma is equivalent to A level, but as it covers only one field, it isn't as versatile for progression. However, it can be an excellent stepping stone into an advanced, higher, or degree apprenticeship, or a full-time university degree course in a related vocational subject. BTEC is a good route if you've already decided your career direction; if you haven't, it isn't.

Why take an apprenticeship?

You can begin an apprenticeship leading to advanced level at age 16, 17 or 18 (and sometimes later), though required (or preferred) entry qualifications will vary with the level, and most STEM-related ones are likely to be at advanced. As with BTEC, this route is advisable only if you have a clear career direction in mind, but some apprenticeships still open up more than others. For instance, if you're good at maths, an apprenticeship in accountancy will take you into a specific line of work, whereas one in business would offer more time to decide whether (and how) to use this ability in employment. It's not advisable to go for the apprenticeship route without a taste of the work environment you're likely to encounter. If your school/college won't offer you work experience, take the initiative and arrange it yourself. Not having done any could place you at a disadvantage come application time.

If you haven't liked school or college, an apprenticeship may seem to offer a fresh start. However, in general, work environments tend to be more demanding than educational ones. You need to be able to cope with a longer working day, (often) a more formal environment, and targets or deadlines to meet, but an apprenticeship should be good if you like to see the relevance of what you're learning and, of course, you'll be earning money, too. Bear in mind that an advanced apprenticeship *may* lead on to a higher or degree one, but there is rarely any guarantee of this.

Why take a higher or degree apprenticeship?

This route is to be recommended only if you've done (or expect to do) well not only in GCSEs, but in A levels or in a BTEC level 3 diploma (in effect, well enough to go to university). This is partly because of the level of competition likely for such opportunities and because studying for a degree (or similar qualification) will be part of the deal. You must show you're up for this, for instance by showing selectors that you've explored and are enthusiastic about the nature of the training, you understand how the organisation involved operates, and the products and services it delivers, and are prepared to undertake demanding study likely to eat into your evenings and weekends. Higher and degree apprenticeships are fairly new, but they seem to offer excellent prospects.

Why take a full-time first degree?

The work-based route to graduation has its advantages, as we've seen, but usually takes significantly longer than the three years typical for full-time courses. So, assuming you want (or need) a degree, how far is speed of the essence? People most concerned about this usually include those who know they'll need a higher degree, too. University-based (i.e. full-time) first degrees in STEM subjects are often considered among the most demanding, with busy days in lectures and laboratory, or engaged in fieldwork, being followed by evening reading and assignments.

Most STEM courses are offered at a healthy range of institutions, so you'll have meaningful choice, though some can be taken only at a handful. This generally reflects a smaller body of professional practitioners and comparably few vacancies each year, factors you should take into account.

Choosing the university route involves making non-academic or career decisions, too, such as whether to study locally (perhaps living at home) or go away, and (if the latter) what kind of accommodation will suit you best. It's important to remember that university can offer much more than the chance to gain an important qualification, and the range of activities and events on offer can contribute positively to the whole experience.

Pioneer in STEM
Tim Berners-Lee (born 1955)

Tim Berners-Lee was born in 1955, to parents who worked on computers, including the Ferranti Mark I, the first commercially built machine. As a child, his interest in electronics was sparked by his model railway and he went to Oxford in 1973, gaining a first-class degree in physics there three years later.

After graduation, he worked for the telecommunications company Plessey, in Dorset, where he helped create typesetting software for printers. Next came a short period at CERN (then the largest internet node in Europe) in Geneva in 1980, followed by some experience in computer networking, before he returned to CERN in 1984 as a Fellow.

Tim Berners-Lee had a vision of a global hyperlinked information system and this began to seem more realistic when in 1988 the first internet connection between Europe and North America was established. In the following year (1989), he was able to present to CERN his plan for a World Wide Web. It differed from other links of that era by enabling a user to link to another resource without any action by the owner of that source. In 1993, CERN announced that the World Wide Web would be free to anyone, with no fees due, and no licensing restrictions.

Though often used without distinction, the terms 'Internet' and 'World Wide Web' are not the same. The first is a global system of interconnected computer networks, the second a global connection of documents and similar resources. A panel of eminent achievers ranked the Web the most important cultural moment in history, describing it as having 'changed the shape of modern life forever'.

Tim Berners-Lee was knighted by the Queen in 2004 and joined the Department of Computer Science at Oxford in 2016. He strongly advocates that the Web should offer 'connectivity with no strings attached' and condemns browsing of users' activities without their consent as an infringement of basic human rights.

Studying abroad

A very big step, but one which many find appealing, is to study abroad. The USA and other English-speaking countries may come first to mind, but their course fees are often prohibitively high. By contrast, a number of European countries have fees very low by British standards, and some charge none at all. Better still, there are literally hundreds (possibly thousands) of STEM-related first and higher degrees offered at European universities which are taught in English. Brexit (see pages 3–4) may have some effect on their availability. If you'd like to explore the option of studying somewhere outside Britain, see *Studying Abroad* (Trotman Education).

Why take a higher degree?

Most people who take a STEM higher degree (usually an MSc or a PhD) do so because they need this to have a serious chance of gaining a post in their preferred specialism. An MSc (normally one year, full-time) may be enough, but most opportunities in research demand a PhD. This normally takes three further years after graduation, so you need to think seriously about it. You need to really prove yourself at undergraduate level, and most successful candidates for a master's or a doctorate hold a First or 2.i class degree. You should also have a real enthusiasm for your chosen topic, as you're likely to be working on it (or something closely related) for some years afterwards, whether in a commercial, academic or research setting.

Why take a foundation course?

Sometimes a student taking non-science A levels becomes attracted to a STEM degree course or career for which his/her current subjects are unsuitable. A possible solution is the Foundation Year (sometimes called Year Zero) which many universities offer. This is not part of any degree course; rather it's a one-year full-time study programme designed to give enough basic knowledge to allow someone completing it to start a STEM-related first degree directly afterwards, at little or no disadvantage. However, good grades in the (non-science) A levels are still required and anyone considering this route should carefully explore the success rate of Year Zero students, and see how they cope generally. One final point – the Foundation Year is not to be confused with foundation degrees described elsewhere, the latter being workplace-oriented and specifically vocational.

Fascinating fact

In 2014, a team of scientists used one of the world's largest airships to explore the atmosphere. Bearing the logo 'Cloud Lab', the ship undertook various experiments, including flying into a cloud to use light radar to calculate its weight. The small cloud it passed through weighed four tons.

Why take a sponsorship?

Sponsorships pre-date apprenticeships in their current form and some are long-established. Most are formal packages featuring many benefits of apprenticeships (at any level), but often additionally attractive or distinctive. Recruits are known as 'sponsees' and may begin a programme during sixth form/college or while at university. Arrangements vary, but in essence the sponsee is paid while studying and works for the sponsoring organisation during college or university holidays (or at least part of them). The employer also pays course fees, but this may be for a specific degree course (e.g. electronic engineering) at a particular university, with which it has links. Some are well-known organisations, including the armed services, whose sponsorships are highly thought of.

Typically, sponsorships are advertised, but you're also free to approach any organisation and ask for one. A well-composed letter stating clearly what you have in mind, accompanied by an informative (and hopefully distinctive) CV would be the way to start. Make sure you research the organisation, to check that what you say ties in with what they do. This route may appeal if you have a good deal of initiative, self-confidence and excellent self-presentation skills on paper and in person.

Conclusion

Researching options and making applications take time. To avoid having to cope with either while revising for important exams, prepare early. From September of the year before entry, educational institutions and training organisations run information events and open their doors, so you can get an idea of where you might want to go several months before decision time. Any work experience should also be completed well before exams. At first, every option may appeal to you, but have a good think and talk with parents and teachers to help narrow these down; you should be able to select two or three options that are within your capabilities and genuinely appeal. Make sure that you're taking into account a recognised route into any course, job or training you're aiming to enter later on.

10 | Personal profiles of STEM employees

Introduction

This chapter offers a picture of eight STEM jobs through the eyes of the four men and four women who do them. These short profiles present each job's typical activities and some of their pros and cons as the tellers see them. Collectively they include many aspects you may expect in STEM-related work. Remember, however, that while the personal angle may breathe more life into the jobs explained below, they are the experiences of individuals and should not make up the sole evidence on which any of them is judged. But the positive features will hopefully inspire you to find out more, while any negative impressions may at least make you think about these jobs more carefully.

 Case study: Angela, biology teacher

I teach biology at a secondary school with a sixth form. Most of my work is with final-year GCSE and A level students. I spend part of each day planning lessons, and making sure any equipment I need for laboratory lessons is available and in good order. You have to give very specific directions to students doing lab work for health and safety reasons – fortunately, biology tends not to be quite as hazardous as chemistry!

Students submit a lot of their work on computer, which means it's easy to mark at home if I haven't time during the school day. I offer as much feedback as I can on a one-to-one basis, especially to my A level students, and particularly if I feel they haven't quite grasped something which I know will also be important later in the syllabus; having said that, it's not always easy to judge whether someone has really understood a concept. Biology is the most popular science by some way among our female students, so the A level group is well balanced gender-wise. This makes it easier to get girls to take seriously the prospect of a career in biology, especially once they've had a university visit.

I like teaching project work on specific topics, which are good for showing the relevance of biology as a subject. Some, like global warming, make it easy to demonstrate how things are interlinked and how collective small changes can lead to major upheavals. I accompany students on at least one field trip each year; the last two have been to a nature reserve near the coast, which offers a good range of flora and fauna. The trips are really useful for getting students to work together and to see how different specialisms can combine to produce useful findings, or an overall picture.

The school has two open evenings each year, which offer chances to attract would-be science sixth-formers, as we're the only one of three local secondary schools offering A levels.

I've been here 12 years and have no ambition to be a head of department or an administrator. I'm an Advanced Skills Teacher and am quite content, salary-wise. It might be nice to be ranked as an Excellent Teacher, but it's not something I'm pushing for. Feeling that I've helped a student towards a real interest in the subject I love is the biggest satisfaction.

 Case study: Geoff, quantity surveyor

I started as a quantity surveyor with my own local authority, but now work for a commercial building contractor. This means being based on a construction site (normally with a Portakabin office) and moving from one project to another. Fortunately I rarely have to travel beyond a radius of about 20 miles, which helps, as I have a young family.

My job involves calculating the cost of building projects, taking account of materials and labour mainly, but of maintenance, too. The bulk of this work is for housing, but on larger projects there can be the occasional one-off structure, like a school, or a library, or a medical centre. We even did a church, once! I do my calculations following the architect's or civil engineer's designs. Being good with figures is important, but you need a knowledge of building methods and of construction law, as well as a realistic sense of the speed work can progress. Health and safety are important, too – I always wear a hard hat on site. Some of the tasks are subcontracted, so I have to ensure we get a good deal on those. Things tend to move along pretty quickly from about April to the end of October, but winter weather can put projects behind, sometimes by a week or more. We've been fairly lucky in recent years, but it's something you do have to allow for.

At school I did A levels, which included maths, then took a degree in quantity surveying, but I know some younger people now taking advanced apprenticeships and a couple of others who qualified after coming in at technician level. I like this firm and plan to stay with them for at least the next few years. Eventually, I'd like to work for myself, though, as an independent consultant – about one in every five quantity surveyors is self-employed.

Fascinating fact

The age of timber in buildings can be calculated very precisely by scientific examination. People who study wood to estimate age are called dendrochronologists.

Case study: Laura, engineering draughtsperson

I work for an engineering firm which manufactures items used in industry. I make the final drawings which the production-line staff refer to. There are actually two stages in the drawing process; the first is known as 'design', which entails producing a scale drawing presenting the general outline, plus a calculation of the number of parts needed, together with their size and weight. The second stage is called the 'detail', which is what I and three of my colleagues do.

The detail stage requires a separate drawing for each part of the manufacturing procedure. Each one in the series has to be very precise, but easy to understand, as the production-line staff rely on it alone. I have to know what machinery they'll be using, and what its capabilities are, as well as the skill levels of the staff themselves. I actually spend a lot of time on the shop floor to find out what I need to know, which includes talking to the operations people. Care and accuracy, and attention to detail are all really important, or you may miss something vital. You must be able to use mathematical formulae and be happy using a calculator. We use CAD technology for the drawings themselves, although the ability to do a quick hand sketch can still sometimes come in handy.

Six of us belong to the drawing team, including Sharon, whom I was at college with. We both took design and technology to NVQ level 2, but wanted a job with a really practical side, as well. We applied for an apprenticeship here and were really surprised when we were both taken on. The training was first-rate, but not easy in the beginning – often having to put in some study following what seemed a long day (after college) – but it was all really interesting. About a year after finishing the apprenticeship, I asked to go part-time, so I work 25 hours a week, rather than 35. This lets me leave early each day, which is really helpful, as my partner works full time and our little boy's only two.

Engineering is still a predominantly male occupation, but Sharon and I have never felt put down by any of the men here and really feel we're valued as much as anyone else. I've no plans to move on, but if I did, I'd still want to be in engineering.

 Case study: Ahmed, pharmaceutical toxicologist

Toxicology is basically finding out how to reduce or eliminate the real or potentially harmful effects of drugs or chemicals. When problems arise, it's usually because a substance has been contaminated in some way. Sometimes the substance itself is fine, though, but it has been misused, like being introduced at too high a dosage.

I work for a pharmaceutical company and medicines are my focus. When a new drug is produced, the first stage of testing for safety is to assess its effects on cells. This is done in the laboratory and called 'in vitro' testing (meaning 'in the glass', i.e. in a test tube). If these results are satisfactory, we move to the next stage, which is with small animals, like mice. If these are okay, too, we finally test on human volunteers. These last two stages are called 'in vivo' testing (meaning 'in life', i.e. in a living thing). We try to keep these to a minimum, which we can do if we already know a lot about the toxicity of a similar drug already in use. This is a job where you have to be very aware of safety procedures and of course ensure that any volunteers are fully informed before agreeing to co-operate with testing.

My first degree was in pharmacology, then I took an MSc degree in toxicology. I did consider going into forensic toxicology (investigating the circumstances of drug use in legal cases), but this work often relates to very sad circumstances, and there can be a lot of hanging around courtrooms, so I decided on the pharmacy side. It's possible to get even more specialised, into areas like immuno-toxicology or neurotoxicology (effects of drugs on the immune and nervous systems), but that would probably entail further study, especially if I wanted to be based in a university or research centre, which does appeal to me. Maybe I'll just have to buckle down and do a PhD!

 Case study: Caroline, laboratory technician

I work in a secondary school with quite a big sixth form. It has specialist status in science, so there's always a push to get good results in these subjects each year. Most of what I know is chemistry-related, but John, the other technician, has a physics background, so our combined science knowledge is quite broad. I liaise with all the science staff, but mainly the head of chemistry. He and the heads of physics and biology usually meet with John and me on Thursdays to raise any issues and authorise any stock orders we'll need over the next week or two. Most meetings are quite short, unless there's something like an OFSTED inspection looming, which needs extra preparation or careful checks, at least. Disposing of lab waste is another regular job, which has to be done carefully with hazardous materials – in a school, health and safety are always high priority.

A lot of my time's spent keeping instruments in good order, and making sure they're in the right place and set up properly for lessons. Even when students are expected to do this themselves, I stand by anyway, just to be sure. The part of the job I actually enjoy most is preparing teaching aids; I often do this for the newer members of staff and sometimes help out in lab sessions.

I didn't go to university, but took the level 3 diploma in laboratory science at college. I've been here nearly four years, but long term I'd like to work in research. A spell in industry might lead me to that, but I'll need a further qualification, probably a degree. I'm hesitating between one in chemistry, which I enjoy, and one in laboratory science, which might be more versatile. I'm only 22, so from a time perspective I'm in no special hurry. The Open University might be an option, especially if they'll give me credit for the work I've done here.

Case study: Peter, forensic scientist

I'm a civilian employee working within a police force and provide scientific evidence for use in courts of law. Obviously I work closely with uniformed officers, but my approach has to be impartial, as what I produce or report can be presented or challenged by the prosecution or the defence. Most of my work relates to police investigations and I analyse evidence mostly collected by their scenes of crime officers. On the occasions I do visit a site it's to offer advice on the collection procedure itself.

Most forensic evidence is physically very small and often has to be examined under a microscope or even an electron microscope. We also use equipment capable of testing lots of samples simultaneously, which is a great timesaver. Often we're looking at things like fibres from clothing, blood or urine samples, and even objects handled during the commission of a crime. The purpose is usually to establish or rule out a link between a suspect and a location and/or victim. The availability of DNA profiling has been a huge step, significantly reducing the chance of error and wrongful conviction. Another technique is gas chromatography; in the aftermath of a fire, this can be used to detect substances such as petrol fumes, which might suggest that the blaze was started deliberately.

When I've finished evaluating the physical evidence, I put my findings in a report to be presented in court. This means it must be clear and (above all) unambiguous, and explain any technical terms so that they can be understood by a jury of non-specialists. Sometimes I'm asked to give evidence in court, which in the beginning I found quite nerve-wracking, but five years on, I take it pretty much in my stride now. Occasionally my court appearances are to do with civil cases rather than criminal cases, like a dispute over responsibility for a road accident, for instance.

My first degree at university was in biology, then I did an MSc in forensic science. TV series have always given this work a more glamorous image than it merits, which partly explains the growth of forensic degree courses, and quite recently an over-production of graduates, which has resulted in very strong competition for jobs. There's no denying that the work can be fascinating, and I like the people I regularly deal with, but in the long term, I'd like to be self-employed as a consultant.

Pioneer in STEM
Alec Jeffreys (born 1950)

When he was only eight, Alec Jeffreys was given a real chemistry set by his father. His enthusiasm was aroused and in time led him to a first-class degree in biochemistry at Oxford. After his doctorate there, he entered the University of Amsterdam as a postdoctoral research fellow, where he and a colleague developed a method for detecting specific genes in humans.

While considering whether to stay on at Amsterdam, he was offered a temporary lecturing post at the University of Leicester. This gave him, at the age of 27, charge of a small laboratory and the assistance of a part-time technician. He was now free to focus on the inherited variation of genes and, specifically, DNA. By examining how genetic variations evolved, he detected 'minisatellites' within the DNA, which were sufficiently differing to provide genetic markers.

In 1984, he arrived at the world's first genetic fingerprint, whose potential value he could see in establishing an individual's identity beyond doubt. The first demonstration of this to reach the public's notice came only the year after, in an immigration case. A paternity legal case soon after strengthened its reputation and two years later ICI (now Astrazeneca) established it on a commercial basis.

It reached its highest news profile, however, when it established one man guilty of a double murder, when someone else would otherwise almost certainly have been convicted. The UK now has a national database of 2.5 million genetic profiles from convicted criminals which police say is one of the most powerful tools in their fight against crime.

In 1994, Alec Jeffreys was knighted for his services to genetics. He continues to work on the ways in which DNA mutates.

Case study: Sunita, zoological scientist

My specialist field is endangered species and I work mainly in zoos and safari parks. When I do fieldwork, it's normally in Africa, though quite recently I contributed to a project on bears, which entailed trips to North America and China. People like me have to look not only at an animal's physiology and behaviour, but its environment, too. When a species becomes endangered, or even extinct, it's hardly ever explained by only a single reason or factor, but rather a combination, which often includes destruction of habitat through such processes as deforestation by logging companies, encroachment on living space by humans, and the introduction of inimical foreign species.

The initial task of a fieldwork expedition is normally to record the range of species within a precise geographical area, usually a fairly small one. This contributes to forming a picture reflecting the locality, but which raises understanding at national and global levels, too. The next step entails minute observation of specific animals, and technology now lets us gather far more data than ever, with miniature cameras and microphones recording every movement and sound. This has contributed enormously to seeing how certain species raise their young. These facilities don't tell us everything, though, and you still have to get close up, which takes patience, as animals are very sensitive and easily spooked.

Observations made in the field aid the survival of the indigenous species, but also improve our understanding and treatment of animals in captivity, which is where my contact with zoos and safari parks comes in. As well as discussing particular species with established staff there, I help to train newcomers and do a limited number of talks to the visiting public. These (I hope) help lay people better to understand and enjoy the animals they see there, but also grasp that the 'wow factor' animals often depend on less spectacular ones and so their well-being is important too.

My remaining time is usually university- or research centre-based. This is where we analyse recordings and do the number-crunching. You need to be good with figures, because statistics form the basis of published research, but also because reliable numbers can drive positive action, including government policy. The laboratory work I do relates to selection and breeding and an exciting area is the reintroduction of species from captivity into the wild – but this has to be really well thought through, and relies on co-operation from all quarters.

I did my first degree in ecology, followed by a PhD in zoology. The work is demanding and involves a lot of travel, but I've had some wonderful encounters with very special animals. I've no wish to be doing anything else.

Case study: David, IT service manager

I work for a computer dealership and organise technical support and advice to customers during and after sales of computer systems. I do some of the technical work myself, as well as organising a support team, who are mainly help desk staff. I quite often visit customers (or potential customers) to demonstrate software or install hardware systems. Sometimes I'll need to point out to organisations that they need additional software for the tasks they want their IT to perform. Once they're happy about the equipment, I'll draw up a service level agreement which ensures ongoing support after sales. We offer the bulk of our advice online, though, or by phone or email. Besides supervising my support team, I liaise with sales staff and our suppliers.

Most technical problems can be sorted out quite quickly, but I discuss any recurring ones with our production and technical managers, because satisfied customers are essential. Most of our help desk staff have been here a while and are very competent. I'm involved with any recruitment, but someone else supervises newcomers' training. However, I deliver a few training sessions myself, usually ones related to 'troubleshooting'. I write training notes for staff, along with technical reports on systems, plus summaries for senior management – these last ones normally on a monthly basis, but occasionally extra ones, like at the end of the financial year, or after introducing a new product or service. From time to time I review the effectiveness of existing systems and help budget and plan for the future, both short- and long-term. Nominally our service is countywide, but most jobs fall within a 15-mile radius, which means travelling time isn't excessive.

I did a BTEC level 3 diploma in IT at college, then an IT management for business degree, something developed in co-operation with some big firms, to be as employer-relevant as possible. I've only been in this job two years and there's scope for me to move up or sideways with the company if I want to. The work is demanding, but very stimulating and I respond quite well to pressure, provided it's not excessive. I enjoy the training duties in particular, and could even see myself becoming a training manager. However, anyone thinking of doing my job should recognise that it's as much about being organised and good with people as knowing about IT.

Conclusion

Despite the broad occupational range these eight profiles represent, certain aspects repeatedly surface within them. These are health and safety, reliance on technology, and having a grasp of details. Most significant, though, is the importance of working successfully with others. In fact, from the largest engineering team project to the most obscure medical research, success in STEM occupations is clearly rooted in collaboration, in contrast to the popular image of the lone pioneer scientist.

11 | Some major STEM employers

Introduction

Once you've got a good idea of the career you'd like, you might want to then see who you might work for. Good opportunities exist within organisations of all sizes, but household name ones (sometimes also called blue chip firms) act as a magnet to many. The purpose of this chapter is to illustrate STEM-related opportunities as they occur within some major employers across a range of industries and services. However confident you may be in your own abilities, though, the competition for what's on offer makes it only sensible also to explore well beyond those featured here.

This chapter offers a brief description of 10 organisations. Some are foreign-owned, or belong to international groups, but all have a significant presence in Britain, and are engaged in STEM-related activities. They offer excellent opportunities for young people, most through well-established programmes. These often start with apprenticeships aimed at 16–17-year-olds, and sometimes progress to graduate level. Some of those employers, however, look to recruit only graduates of a high calibre, and sometimes in a specific subject or within a narrow range. All these organisations have informative and attractive websites which provide useful details.

Two things which you'll quickly notice are the size of the organisations featured and their spread of opportunities. These are not unrelated, since the more products or services, the larger the likely numbers of employees and outlets. All these require organisation, and staff expert in business, finance and marketing, for instance, are needed in significant numbers. Where operations are international (true of nearly all those here) staff familiar with foreign languages and cultures have an important role. The majority of these wider opportunities occur at graduate level and are commonly open to applicants of any discipline. A STEM degree is a helpful background, but could still let you train and function in a different line which attracts you. So having a STEM degree needn't commit you to a STEM job, while a non-STEM degree may well still let you work for a STEM organisation.

Pioneer in STEM
Marie Curie (1867-1934)

Born Maria Sklodowska in Poland, the youngest of five children, Marie Curie grew up in modest circumstances. Her hopes of becoming a teacher were punctured when her mother died and her father could no longer support her. Instead, she became a governess, but read and studied avidly and in 1891, at the age of 24, enrolled at the Sorbonne in Paris to study physics and maths. Three years later, she met Pierre Curie, a scientist who worked in the city, and they married soon after.

Together they became researchers at the School of Chemistry and Physics in Paris, where they also began their pioneering investigations of the invisible rays given off by the element uranium. Like the also recently detected X-rays, these had been seen to penetrate solid objects. Marie noticed that samples of material called pitchblende (which contains uranium ore) were much more radioactive than even pure uranium. She knew there must be another substance in the pitchblende, but one existing only in very small quantities. Convinced that they had discovered a new element, Marie and Pierre succeeded in extracting a black powder 300 times as radioactive as uranium, which they called polonium.

But this was not the end of the story, as the liquid residue from this reductive process contained something even more radio-active, existing in a tinier proportion still. Through heavy physical as well as intellectual labour, Marie and Pierre finally produced a very small quantity of an extremely radioactive material which they called radium. During the process, both suffered (then) unexplained illness and tiredness, which today we recognise as early symptoms of radiation sickness.

In 1903, Marie and Pierre and another scientist shared the Nobel Prize for Physics, the same year as she received her doctorate in the subject. Tragically, Pierre was killed in a street accident three years later. Marie succeeded him as professor at the Sorbonne, and in 1911 earned a second Nobel Prize after devising a method of measuring radioactivity. During World War I, she developed small, mobile X-ray units to help in diagnosing combat injuries, and was a director of the Red Cross Radiologist Service.

Marie Curie's work came to be most significant in relation to cancer treatments and, by the time of her death in 1934, she had attained worldwide recognition.

Deloitte

Deloitte is the collective name for members of Deloitte Touche Tohmatsu Ltd (DTTL), a UK private company. DTTL members operate worldwide, each one conforming to the laws and professional regulations of the country in which it's located.

The organisation offers financial services, mostly in the form of auditing, consulting, financial advising, risk management and taxation. Its British arm offers intermediate apprenticeships for applicants with five good grades at GCSE (or equivalent), and advanced apprenticeships for those with these plus quite good A levels (or equivalent). There are insights workshops aimed at undergraduates on target for a 2.i degree at a British university, while internships are available through its Summer and Vacation Scheme to those further on in their career. Graduates (from First class to 2.ii) are considered depending on their professional specialisms, or where they'd like to be placed, but some opportunities do require a specific degree subject.

KPMG

KPMG was founded in 1987 through the merger of a Dutch company and a British one. Like Deloitte, it's regarded as one of the 'big four' accounting organisations, and is similarly made up of firms based in different countries. Their areas of activity are audit, tax, advisory work and enterprise, the last of which helps privately owned businesses to achieve their ambitions. The company has 20 offices nationwide, with opportunities for young people at all of them. KPMG's website notes the range and spread of changes in the world of work, and how it can help employers to react positively to these, highlighting the importance of harnessing technology and investing in innovation.

The KPMG 360° programme is a vocational apprenticeship allowing entrants to work in different areas of the organisation and gain professional qualifications along the way. The programme is offered at three levels – foundation, technician and professional.

KPMG Discovery is for Year 12 students, and offers three-day and five-day programmes in which participants undertake a series of business challenges and research tasks designed to develop key skills the firm needs. The One Year Business Placement Programme is paid work experience intended as the 'filling' in a sandwich degree, while Launch Pad is for graduates (or those about to graduate), a 2.i degree in any discipline being expected.

Jaguar Land Rover

The Jaguar and Land Rover firms were taken over by the Indian automobile giant Tata Motors in 2008, but only became a single company officially in 2013. It's now the largest car manufacturer business in the UK, combining a luxury saloon/sports brand with an early four-wheel drive one. The Land Rover vehicle (inspired by the American Jeep) appeared in the years soon after World War II, with the Range Rover being launched in 1970, and is still popular today. The company's activities are wide-ranging, but are essentially a combination of engineering, finance and marketing. The engineering sector is itself split into subdivisions such as product, manufacturing and commercial, with supply chain and logistics, marketing, IT and finance also represented.

This variety is reflected it its recruitment, with advanced and degree-level apprenticeships running over four and six years respectively. Undergraduates in their penultimate year of study are eligible for bursaries to cover work experience placements lasting from three months to a year. Jaguar Land Rover is keen to attract female graduates and offers a programme which includes one-to-one mentoring from one of its women engineers.

AstraZeneca UK

AstraZeneca is a British-Swedish multinational pharmaceutical and biopharmaceutical company, which has its main headquarters in Cambridge. It's active in more than 100 countries, with growing markets in China, Brazil, Mexico and Russia. Its worldwide workforce numbers nearly 60,000, with its seven centres in the UK employing 7,000.

The company's website declares its purpose as being 'to get effective new medicines to those who need them as quickly and safely as possible'. To this end, it devotes £4 billion annually to six areas of therapy or treatment – cancer, cardiac, metabolic, respiratory, inflammatory and autoimmunity, while also remaining active in infection and neuroscience. Besides the wide spectrum of science opportunities the company's role generates, it also offers careers in engineering and IT.

Forestry Commission

In England, the Secretary of State for Environment and Rural Affairs is responsible for public forests, and the organisation is called the Forestry Commission, which employs over 2,000 people. Within it is the Forest Research Agency, which provides high-quality data and analysis through its scientific research and surveys. These inform policy and practice, as well as promoting high standards of sustainable forest management. Its research over the past five years has been focused on four main areas:

1. Pests and diseases (including projects on acute oak decline, grey squirrels and socio-economic aspects of tree health)
2. Climate change (including investigations on urban trees and brownfield sites)
3. Ecosystem services (including programmes on forest hydrology, genetic conservation and soil sustainability)
4. Forest management (including examinations of conifer breeding, seed science, private landowners and tree and wood properties).

The Forestry Commission offers apprenticeships to school leavers, but these focus more on practical activities than STEM-related ones. However, it does offer sandwich placements to undergraduates and has a graduate division programme. For those holding or aspiring to a 2.i class science degree, research-oriented work would be an option.

Office for National Statistics (ONS)

The ONS is the UK's largest independent producer of official statistics. It collects, analyses and disseminates reliable figures about Britain's economy, society and population. One example of the scale of its data is the Inter-Departmental Business Register, which holds information on over two million of the country's enterprises.

Statistical officers in the ONS typically work within a team. They develop statistical tools for future data collection; improve ways of collecting data via surveys; use administrative data for statistical reports; identify customer needs and ensure data for them is fit for purpose; interpret statistical analysis for policy development, and help build confidence in statistics generally by applying the official code of practice. Those appointed normally have at least a class 2.ii degree in a numerate discipline like maths or economics, which has included some training in statistics.

Two other posts within the ONS are data scientist and fast stream statistician. A degree in maths, economics, IT or computer science is normally needed, but at class 2.i for the second job, which is described on its website as 'the flagship training scheme for future statistical leaders'. Its responsibilities include preparing statistical briefings for the press and senior colleagues, and even representing the UK abroad.

BAE Systems

The registered office of BAE Systems is in London, but the company has more than 15 other UK sites where a wide range of activities take place. Some of these are for commercial organisations, mainly in electronics for IT and security systems, but the bulk is military-related. It designs, manufactures and supports combat vehicles on land, and both surface ships and submarines for maritime defence.

The company offers numerous opportunities at apprenticeship, undergraduate and graduate levels. The apprenticeship menu is especially long, featuring roles such as aerospace engineering and software development, aircraft maintenance and support, combat systems engineering, IT, electronic systems and nuclear systems, as well as steelmaking and welding.

For undergraduates on target for a 2.i class degree, it offers a 12-week Summer Internship programme, enabling them to undertake tasks which make a genuine contribution, while earning a salary. For graduates with a 2.i degree in a STEM subject, the best options lie in three areas – engineering, delivery management and consultancy.

IBM

IBM is the largest technology and consulting employer in the world. It operates in 170 countries, including Britain. Its chief expertise lies in IT-based facilities, which include mobile devices, security and cloud facilities, analytics and the internet. Its analytics function is to improve its customers' business functions by telling them what problems they're likely to encounter.

Health is another area where IBM makes a notable contribution, by helping people take better care of themselves. Its technology is capable of prompting valuable insights by rapidly surveying large quantities of health-related data. IBM's Watson Health division has collaborated with Pfizer to help the company accelerate its researches in immuno-oncology (using the body's immune system to better fight cancer).

IBM's technology roles include acting as security specialists, technology solutions experts, technology consultants, software developers, software consultants and technical writers. The organisation offers a range of opportunities in STEM-related work via its apprenticeship and higher apprenticeship programmes. These include its Extreme Blue Summer Apprenticeship, a 12-week paid work experience programme for undergraduates, allowing them to engage in high-profile projects, and (also for undergraduates) its Futures scheme, which involves a 12-month paid gap year. It also offers graduate-entry opportunities.

The NHS

Founded in 1948 by the then Health Minister, Aneurin Bevan, the NHS is the publicly funded national healthcare system for the UK. It's said to be the largest employer in Europe, with an annual budget of over £100 billion. It offers an extremely wide spectrum of jobs, details of which are given on its excellent careers website. Many of these require some STEM subject qualifications, especially those in the sciences bracket.

Everyone recognises jobs like doctor, dentist, nurse, physiotherapist or radiographer, which fall under the NHS umbrella, but so do many little-known ones. These may be less familiar partly because they entail relatively little contact with patients or the public, but the jobs themselves require deep scientific expertise. Some of these areas are:

Anatomic toxicity	–	detecting and measuring potentially harmful chemicals for the diagnosis and prevention of poisoning.
Anatomic pathology	–	processing, examining and diagnosing surgical specimens.
Cellular science	–	identifying abnormalities and interpreting these in relation to patients.
Clinical immunology	–	studying the immune system to help treat allergies and diseases like cancer and AIDS.

Genomics	–	studying genes and how alterations can change how proteins function and are produced.
Histopathology	–	analysing samples of tissue microscopically.
Histocompatibility and immunogenetics	–	testing to support stem cell and organ transplantation.
Reproduction science	–	providing solutions to infertility.
Virology	–	studying viral infections, such as hepatitis and HIV.

Opportunities in these and others are normally offered at both technician and professional level.

National Oceanographic Centre (NOC)

The NOC is based at Southampton and is a centre for research, teaching and technology development in ocean and earth sciences. It was founded in 1995 by the University of Southampton and the National Environment Research Council (NERC), the latter being its owner. It's linked with the Proudman Oceanographic Laboratory at the University of Liverpool, with which it shares facilities and collaborates on research projects from which joint publications emerge.

The NOC undertakes research in five specialist areas: marine geoscience, marine physics and ocean climate, marine systems modelling, ocean biogeochemistry and ecosystems, and ocean technology and engineering. Southampton is the home port for its two purpose-built research ships, RRS *Discovery* and RRS *James Cook*, and three smaller vessels.

The NOC also has multipurpose aquarium facilities, including tanks which mimic habitats such as rock pools and seagrass beds, and pressurised ones which permit the study of deep-sea organisms. It undertakes what it terms 'integrated ocean research and technology development from the coast to the deep ocean', and is committed to ocean observation, mapping and survey, data management and scientific advice. To make its proper contribution to knowledge, research must be integrated, and the NOC works with partners to meet the challenges imposed by changes in sea levels, the ocean's role in climate change, simulating and predicting the behaviour of the oceans through computer modelling, and the future of the Arctic Ocean.

The NOC employs over 500 staff, most of them scientists, engineers and technologists, many of them leaders in their field.

Some staff are pure researchers, while others develop the sophisticated machines they use, or operate the ships by which they reach the areas and habitats they observe. Most employment opportunities are for people qualified at least to degree level in a STEM subject, and often at postgraduate level in a particular one.

 Fascinating fact

In 1960, Jacques Piccard and Don Walsh descended to the bottom of the deepest part of the ocean, the Challenger Deep in the Mariana Trench in the Pacific, where the water is nearly seven miles deep. They achieved this in the bathyscaphe submarine *Trieste*, which used gasoline and electromagnetically controlled iron pellets as ballast.

Conclusion

The employers featured in this chapter have been selected because their size and range of work reflect many interesting STEM developments nationally and internationally. They also show that even the largest organisations willingly recruit not only graduates and postgraduates with excellent records, but also 16- to 18-year-olds for their apprenticeships. However, much smaller concerns also offer proven programmes with very good prospects. Of course, there is status attached to work or training with a household name, but competition for places is going to be greater. For every big organisation you choose to approach, ensure you have at least two or three small to medium ones on your list.

12| Preparation and application for STEM careers

Introduction

If you've reached this point in the book, you'll have read a lot of information and hopefully absorbed a good deal of it. However, you may feel that choosing a STEM career, job or training, then tailoring an application good enough to get a place, still leaves you a lot to do.

This chapter is designed to show that with time, care and determination, you can successfully do both the preparation and application stages in manageable stages. Even if you're not yet sure about a STEM career, it will show you how to discover whether this sector might be suitable for you. Or if you can already see yourself in one of the areas already described, it will show you how to maximise your chances of achieving this, even in competition with promising candidates.

And if you're lying between these extremes – knowing your strengths in STEM subjects, feeling enthusiastic about a particular activity, but still with some exploring to do – this chapter is for you, too.

Getting started

The most likely way to make career decisions which you'll regret later is by rushing them. One thing likely to prompt this is people you know who seem to have already made up their minds, and have their futures all worked out. Don't be misled. Lots of the people who sound decided aren't really, but if they are, this needn't cause you to speed up your own process. Provided you're taking useful steps at a pace you find comfortable, you'll increasingly find the direction that's right for you.

In contrast to people tempted into hasty career decisions, some are frightened to start exploring at all. There are various reasons for this. One may be a nervousness that no career at all will suit you, so it's better not to know this. Another may be a fear that the work environment will be disagreeable, involving less-than-easy tasks performed to sharp deadlines for unsympathetic supervisors. This is only a possibility, but the more effort you put into exploring study, training and work you think you'll like, the less chance you'll have this negative experience. Where certain fears seem justified by knowledge or experience rather than unfounded anxiety, the more likely you'll be to take firm steps to avoid them altogether.

So let's assume you're not unduly anxious, nor in a mad rush, but interested at some level in a STEM-related career – what can you do to get things moving?

Careers education

Some years ago, schools and the government recognised the value of careers education programmes. This resulted in most schools providing their students with a careers library, work experience programmes and classroom sessions covering general career topics, such as interview skills and CV writing; there was also input on well-known and popular occupations, sometimes from visiting speakers. Sadly, and for a variety of reasons, the funding for much of this was reduced or withdrawn, leaving few schools able to continue this provision. However, with ever-growing evidence emerging of students making poor decisions, many institutions are rebuilding the careers edifice which was so valued and useful. Let's hope your school/college either never lost its programme, or is reviving it in the way described. If so, make the most of what's offered – a well-presented careers lesson can (and should) be informative, stimulating and entertaining. Don't think that careers doesn't matter because it's not an assessed subject – in the long run it may benefit you as much as any of your academic ones.

Talking to STEM subject teachers

Careers lessons or programmes are usually delivered by a member of staff with this responsibility. However, you might consider also exploring STEM careers through those who teach related subjects, such as physics, maths, chemistry, biology and technology. Some of them may make a point of talking to groups of their students about the careers related to their specialist subjects. What they say will probably be worth hearing, but remember that (however much they like their subject) they are not careers specialists. This is not to belittle what they tell you, only to recommend that you check any information or advice, preferably through an independent source, such as the website of a professional association. The working world changes very quickly and many staff, very busy just being teachers, haven't always time to keep abreast of it.

However, if they can refer you to someone they know working in a STEM job, this may lead to a useful conversation, or even a visit or work experience, something we'll talk about later in this chapter.

Information gathering

Once upon a time, someone wanting information about a particular career might have to rely on a single source only, or, for the more obscure occupations, perhaps no more than a leaflet several years old. Things could hardly be more different now, with an abundance of material, most of it online. Even so, you're still left with two challenges – how to find the most useful-looking material, and how to know you can trust it. Chapter 13 features books, magazines and websites which are very informative, but ahead of that it's worth offering a few pointers on quality, quantity and reliability.

With so much careers information available, you may gorge on it well beyond your mental appetite. This may result in you getting overloaded and bored, which could discourage you from further exploration in future. Quality and quantity are related here, since a little information taken on board is far preferable to a lot which doesn't really register.

Setting manageable targets

The earlier you begin to look for careers information, the more likely you'll find it in easily digestible amounts. This is because the publishers of material aimed at, say, 14- to 16-year-olds know it has to be attractively presented and punchy to make an impact on students, many of whom will still be window shopping. In introductory material or careers manuals, for instance, entries on individual jobs may only take up one or two paragraphs. This may be all you need at the outset, since even where you have some focus (e.g. work using physics), you'll still need a basic understanding of a range of jobs. This should be easy if you're quite self-disciplined, but if you're not, setting yourself a modest target, like reading a short article on one STEM job each day, will guarantee that you're a good deal more clued up at the end of a fortnight than you were at the beginning. You'll be aware not only of job content, entry requirements and training routes, but also some of the common terminology of scientific, mathematical and technical work. Some of these may already be familiar, but look at the ones which aren't. Additionally, have a chat with any fellow students also exploring STEM careers – you might learn a good deal from one another.

Paper versus technology

Most people now have devices which allow them to look at information at home, or on a tablet or smartphone. All the same, many students say they like using paper resources. One reason is that it's often easier to locate some small piece of information using a reference-book index, for instance, than scrolling down a poorly labelled website. If schools and colleges have a careers library it's likely to be small, but most of these still feature leaflets, booklets and some well-established reference books. Even when small, the library space is often somewhere you can discreetly discuss how best to use information facilities, and discover which ones your fellow students find most useful. Locate your school's or college's careers library (or careers section within a larger resource area) and check when you can use it – sometimes each year group has priority on a given weekday.

Who can you trust?

The last paragraph partly answers the first of the two challenges mentioned at the beginning – how to find the most useful-looking material. Let's now look at the second one – how to know you can trust what you find. The most reliable careers materials are generally those produced by organisations with nothing to gain by presenting a biased picture, which are typically educational or careers publishers. Evidence of their impartiality is usually reflected in the equal space they devote to different occupations and entry routes, without promoting any particular employer, university or training body.

This is not to say that other materials aren't valuable. However, if you first look at the independent sources, you'll be more likely to spot any exaggerations on employer websites or in brochures. Don't be unduly suspicious, though – most are not trying to fool you – but exercising some caution will help keep your expectations realistic. Nevertheless, there comes a point where familiarity with a recruiter's own information is vital, as lacking this is likely to count heavily against you in a job interview or other selection exercise. This is equally important for entry to higher education, as universities say a great deal about course content and relevance, to ensure students know exactly what they're applying for.

Work 'tasting'

Work experience and work 'tasting' can be a great help in making career decisions. For the purposes of this book, though, let's first make a clear distinction between them. Work 'tasting' means a period of less than a week spent on an employer's premises. It may include some practical tasks, but what you learn is more likely to occur through observation and talking to staff. The placement may be for an individual, but may also take place as a small group exercise, a good deal of its value being gained by discussing it afterwards with the others who attend. You may well go to more than one such session to compare different organisations or occupations.

Pioneer in STEM
Marie Stopes (1880-1958)

Marie Stopes was a pioneer woman in the field of science. Her parents belonged to the British Association for the Advancement of Science and her interest in the subject was stimulated when, as a teenager, she accompanied them to its meetings. She attended University College London, where she studied botany and geology, graduating with a first-class BSc degree in 1902. Soon after, she was awarded the DSc (Doctor of Science) degree by London, the youngest person in Britain to receive it, and in 1904, her PhD by the University of Munich.

Later in 1904, she became the first female academic at the University of Manchester. Ostensibly, her lectureship was in botany, but her real interest lay in palaeobotany, the study of fossil plants. At Kew Gardens, she did research into carboniferous plants and in 1907 explored fossil plants in coal mines in Japan, while at the Imperial University, Tokyo, following this in 1910 with geological fieldwork in Canada. That year, her book Palaeontology, an introduction to the subject for non-scientists, was published with considerable success.

Marie returned to University College London, but left in 1920 in order to increase her already strong commitment to the promotion of birth control. The organisation she founded was the Society for Constructive Birth Control and Racial Progress. The clinic with which she was involved was staffed by nurses and supported by visiting doctors.

Stopes was a proponent of eugenics (the genetic improvement of a race) and some of her views, controversial even in her day, we would find offensive now (though possibly for different reasons). However, there can be no denying her place in any science 'hall of fame' as an academic of great ability also powerfully active in promoting women's rights. The scientific classification scheme which she devised for coal is still in use today.

Work experience

By comparison, work experience is a period of at least a week at a time or in total. A continuous placement arranged through school would be unlikely to exceed a fortnight, but one afternoon a week over an academic year (easier in sixth form or college) would total over three weeks' experience. A good deal of the learning here would come about largely through practical activities, hopefully ones tailored to provide as real a sample as possible. You're more likely to benefit by doing things which make even a small contribution, and this is more easily achieved within some workplaces than others. For instance, in a STEM context, the use of dangerous engineering machinery or hazardous laboratory substances may mean opportunities are limited. Good communications in advance of a placement will ensure that the organisation will know what you hope to gain from the experience, and so can do its best to provide this.

Early contact with employers

Of the four avenues which STEM represents, engineering has the highest proportion of non-graduate entrants, who undertake most of their initial training with apprentice or employee status. This reflects no inferiority among either entrants or their employers, but rather the excellent apprenticeship tradition within that sphere. This means that even students in years 10 and 11 could benefit significantly from work experience with such an employer, an offer of training following GCSEs being a real possibility. While they too should be encouraged to engage in work 'tasting' pre-GCSE, students more attracted by the science, maths and technology avenues may benefit more from work experience placements in years 12 and 13, including (possibly) being taken more seriously by the employer involved.

Events

For most students, the three preparatory activities discussed so far can be ongoing. There are also careers events, some national, some regional and some local. Many of these are regulars, occurring annually (sometimes more often) at venues such as universities, colleges or conference centres. A large space is usually needed, as many feature invited organisations (which normally have a stand staffed by represen-tatives) or speakers (who can address groups of between 50 and 100, and often do this more than once during the event).

Large and regular events

A perennial favourite is the National Careers Guidance Show, which takes place at a handful of venues nationwide, as its name suggests. Excellent presentations are made on careers topics, with a wide range of employers represented, some of them STEM-related. Events of comparable size are occasionally run by STEM employers or bodies, sometimes with several working together. Engineering is a notable one, while excellent science opportunities feature within medical-related events, such as those in the NHS.

University departmental open days

Increasing in frequency and popularity are the open days run by the science departments of universities. Most last just a day, but some two, and they may be ticketed, to keep numbers manageable. This means visitors will have much more chance to discuss courses and careers with academic staff, and see close up what's involved in particular fields, including how equipment is used, and how long-term strategies (such as accommodating climate change) are formed. Departmental students are usually involved, so you can more easily picture yourself engaged on projects similar to theirs in the near future.

Taster courses/summer schools

A superior version of the higher education visit just described are university taster courses, sometimes also called summer schools. Most occur during the long school or college holidays at the end of Year 12, and can last up to a week. Places can usually be booked from January and it's worth reserving one well in advance as they're very popular. You're likely to find this sort of event especially valuable if the careers support in your own school or college is limited. This shows the value of starting early when considering university, as some departments may favour applicants who've shown initiative by attending events like this. It also adds a strong point on the personal statement section of your university application (UCAS) form.

College/Sixth form open evenings

Colleges and sixth forms hold open evenings that are very useful to students about to choose A levels or BTEC vocational courses. Besides the information offered as a matter of course, you're likely to derive most benefit from these (and any other events) if you have questions to ask. This may need some thought, but it's always good to ask about what recent students have done afterwards, in terms of university places and jobs. Also, colleges and sixth forms are keen to advertise exam pass rates. These can be close to 100%, and therefore seem impressive, but ask about the percentages of students earning grade B or above, as this may be a better indicator of the quality of teaching.

Training agency and employer events

Training agencies and employers which run their own apprenticeship programmes also offer familiarisation sessions, which local schools are usually invited to. A single provider covering several career areas may run its own, or a number of specialist providers may combine to make a collective one. Many are early in the school autumn term, allowing students plenty of time to consider their findings there before applying. Such events often persuade students who might otherwise have drifted into full-time post-16 study without a second thought, to opt for a work-based route instead.

Your own decisions

At these kinds of events, you're likely to be offered some very attractive material or information by people whose polished presentations or invitations to apply can be very persuasive. However, do remember that this is *your* future, and the only person entitled to make the final decision about what you do or where you do it is you. This is not to criticise these events or anyone at them, or parents, teachers or friends there to support you. But take as much time as you reasonably can, then make a decision which you feel is your own.

Who can help?

Some of the ways in which school staff can help their students have been mentioned already, but other people, too, can be of considerable assistance. An interview with a careers adviser in Year 11 is now rarely automatic, other than for special needs students. Nevertheless, the fact that a careers adviser visits the school may mean that some additional ones can be seen on request, and you should ask your form tutor or careers teacher if you want an appointment. Qualified careers advisers are knowledgeable about the full range of occupations and the routes into them, including degree and postgraduate qualifications. Most will reinforce any information or advice they offer during an interview by writing you a career action plan. This serves as a useful reminder of important facts, or things to do, as well as helping you discuss the interview with your teachers or parents if you want to.

Your parent(s)/guardian(s) can also be a strong support. They're unlikely to be careers experts, but may have studied to quite a high level, or be able to tell you important features of working life based on their own employment histories. They can also offer support on specific occasions, like accompanying you to an interview (if you'd like them to). If they're wise, they'll also appreciate that you're trying to make judgments about yourself, as well as evaluating the information and impressions you receive, and won't press you to make important decisions until you're ready. Very often, though, they can offer helpful reminders of things to do, or draw your attention to events you might otherwise have overlooked or forgotten. Try not to be impatient if they seem to nag a little at times – they just want the best for you.

Making a timetable

There are two reasons why you may get by without making any sort of timetable for your preparations. One is that sometimes material you come across (such as college or sixth form prospectuses) sets out what you should have done, and by when, and highlights useful events such as their own open days. The second reason is that you yourself feel you've such a good grasp of the situation as not to need any prompts – however, few students can honestly say that. Nevertheless, suggested timetables are necessarily general, and don't take account of what stage you're at.

Planning a year ahead

Any plans you make needn't look ahead more than about 12 months. This is because what you learn and achieve in trying to follow one will almost certainly influence you later, so committing yourself to anything beyond a year in the future is probably unnecessary and could be misguided. Let's look now at two sample plans, one for a Year 11 student, and one for a Year 12. We'll assume each is for someone confident of getting quite good academic results, but undecided whether to go for an academic route or a vocational one. Each has some interest in STEM, but as yet no commitment to related study or occupation. First, the Year 11 student:

September	–	Attend open evening of local college; read up on careers using chemistry.
October	–	Attend school trip to apprenticeship event at local conference centre; read up on careers using physics.
November	–	Attend open evenings of two local sixth forms, one very nearby, the other farther away, but with better reputation; read up on careers using maths.
December	–	Consider what you've discovered from events and seeking so far; discuss these with your parent(s) or guardian(s).
January	–	Discuss your likely GCSE grades with teaching staff in the light of mock exam results; ask for an interview with the school's careers adviser.
February	–	Ensure applications to local sixth forms and colleges have been submitted; read up on careers in engineering and technology.
March	–	Attend open days of local training providers specialising in engineering and technology, and apply to two; attend college interview.
April	–	Attend sixth form interviews; contact local employer regarding possibility of STEM-related work experience placement in the summer.
May	–	GCSE exams; receive offer (conditional on GCSE grades) from college and preferred sixth form – accept both.
June	–	More GCSE exams; receive conditional offer from second-choice apprenticeship provider – accept.
July	–	Work experience placement of two weeks with local STEM employer; consider which of three 'accepted' offers to actually take up in September.
August	–	Decide on vocational course in engineering at local college as post-16 destination, particularly in light of excellent work experience placement; good exam results – place confirmed.

Dealing with developments

Notice that even this very brief plan takes account of the increasing need to make decisions as you progress. Aa good plan doesn't remain a skeleton, but gains flesh as you become wiser and more knowledgeable, and as others make decisions about you which you must react to. The example here is also a reminder that you may have to make some big decisions while you're busy with serious revision or exams. Taking things one at a time, and waiting until you've received the responses to all your applications, is likely to ease a good deal of the stress most students experience at this stage. As the plan also shows, it's quite reasonable to accept all offers until you've heard from everyone. However, once you've decided where you really want to go, have the courtesy to inform the organisations which you're no longer interested in, as this allows them to offer your place to someone else. Now, let's look at a comparable plan for a school Year 12 student taking STEM A level subjects:

September	–	Find careers resources in school, which may be in a different place to any used in Year 11.
October	–	Attend school trip to apprenticeship event at local conference centre.
November	–	Attend parents' evening to assess initial progress in each subject. Make a note of any areas which need improvement.
December	–	Arrange interview with careers adviser in school or at local careers centre. Take note of recommendations on resulting careers action plan.
January	–	Read up on careers related to your two best subjects (chemistry and biology). Attend school talk on higher education.
February	–	Begin to look at university prospectuses/websites for courses which combine chemistry and biology. Compare those for pure science with vocational ones (e.g. forensic science, environmental science). Apply for university taster course/summer school.
March	–	Visit two local universities whose websites and reputations attract you, on their open days. Have specific questions ready to ask.
April	–	Arrange a week's work experience for summer vacation with a local STEM employer undertaking biology- or chemistry-related activities. Read up on careers related to courses seen on two university visits.
May	–	Visit two more universities a little further from home. Focus on courses not seen during earlier two visits.
June	–	Attend local careers event on applying to university. Summer exams.
July	–	Arrange follow-up interview with careers adviser. Refine intended degree course and university choices in light of this. Discuss with parent(s)/guardian(s)/school staff.
August	–	Undertake work experience as arranged with STEM employer involved in activities related to intended degree course. Hopefully confirmation of career direction and higher education plan as a result, before start of Year 13 in September.

Making a plan that suits you

These two sample plans offer no more than a sense of how a real one might look. It's often useful in constructing one first to mark in events beyond your control, such as the dates of open days. This gives you full scope to then pencil in ones where you can use your discretion. Bear in mind that careers advisers are often booked up, so make any appointments a week or two ahead of when you want to see them. Tasks described in a general way here, such as reading up on careers in chemistry, may have to be more specific, targeting particular reference books or websites, for instance. Knowing what these sources are ahead of using them will save time, and hopefully make it more enjoyable in itself. Be honest with yourself about the kind of plan you'll actually work to, then draw it up yourself. This is much better than someone (however capable) doing it for you. Don't do without a plan altogether – having one at least gives you the best chance of covering all the angles.

Applying for sixth forms, colleges or training

Perhaps the most important thing for any student in Year 11 to realise is that no progression beyond it is automatic. To people accustomed from the age of five to uninterrupted educational progression, this can come as a surprise. Even within the same school, moving from the GCSE year into the sixth form usually depends (exam results apart) on completing an application form and a successful interview. Where many of the staff already know you, this may be a straightforward and fairly stress-free experience, especially if you're strong academically. Nevertheless, tutors on STEM-related courses will still expect you to express sound reasons for choosing their subjects, and to have some idea of where these might lead you.

There's no reason to think that the selection process for somewhere unfamiliar (such as a college or apprenticeship provider) will be difficult. However, you may have to apply by a deadline, and undertake some form of written selection or aptitude test, as well as being interviewed by one or two people who don't know you or your strengths. It's worth doing some serious preparation to avoid undue anxiety which prevents you doing yourself justice.

Most educational institutions and employers still offer a paper application form, but many now prefer candidates to complete it online, as it helps processing, including keeping applicants up to date of their progress. However, these electronic versions are often significantly longer than paper ones, requiring more thought and information. You need to know this, as it may affect the number or quality of the applications you make, and, in turn, your chances of being accepted.

Finally, if you're applying for popular courses or training, try to find out the likely strength of the competition. Well-respected apprenticeship programmes with household-name employers can attract dozens of applicants for every place, and this may be equally true for limited scholarship places at some sixth form colleges or independent schools. For these, you may need excellent self-presentation skills and more than the five good GCSE passes that are normally sufficient.

Fascinating fact

There are now nearly 15,000 centenarians alive in Britain today. The oldest person ever recorded, Jeanne Calment, a Frenchwoman, died in 1997, aged 122. People who study ageing are called gerontologists.

Applying for higher education

The application process for higher education is a good deal more demanding. Although you only submit a single form, the preparation and thought needed to complete it well outweigh the work of several applications to post-16 organisations. We've already covered the recommended preparations, but it's certainly also worth describing the form here and how best to present yourself on it.

The UCAS form

The body supervising the higher education application process in Britain each year is called the Universities Central Admissions Service (UCAS). The vast majority of applicants submit the online version of the form, which UCAS forwards to the (up to five) institutions which you can apply to. There are three main parts to the form: factual information, much of it covering GCSE results and A level (or equivalent) subjects being taken; a personal statement, saying mainly why you've opted for the courses you've chosen; and a supporting statement from your school or college, written by tutors who know and teach you. Relatively few applicants are interviewed as part of selection, so most will be judged solely on the contents of their form, which highlights its importance.

The personal statement

There are tight limits on the length of the personal statement and strict deadlines by which UCAS must receive your form, and (later) your decisions regarding any offers of places made to you. Most students need at least some help to write a strong personal statement and may require a good deal. The deadline for submission to UCAS is 15 January of the year of intended entry to university, with some important exceptions, including applications to Oxford and Cambridge (usually three months earlier). To have enough time to offer help to every student needing it, your tutors may ask for your completed parts of the form well before Christmas, in order to write a good enough reference to impress the university selectors. In the light of this, it's well worth making sure you starting preparing early, as described in the sample Year 12 plan.

Conclusion

Perhaps the biggest challenge in the whole business of preparation and application is just getting started. Once you've begun, you'll learn a lot of interesting things, not just concerning jobs or courses, but about yourself. This will create momentum and you'll become eager to know more as you increasingly picture yourself in a work or study setting where you feel you belong. You'll probably also find you needn't follow every recommendation in this chapter and that some you do take less time than expected (though some may take more). Talking to people is sure to help, too – some may even admit to mistakes which help you steer clear of similar ones.

13 | STEM information sources

Introduction

A book of this general scope and limited length can offer no more than an introduction to the career opportunities within a field as broad as STEM. Nevertheless, it will have achieved something if reading up to this point has left you feeling you want to explore STEM careers further.

The purpose of this chapter is to show how you can find reliable information that may be helpful in choosing a STEM-related job, course or training. It draws attention to different formats, with tips on how to find the most useful information quickly. It highlights outstanding publications or websites, and the importance of choosing material pitched at the right level. It cites popular, well-established TV and radio programmes which address STEM issues, some on specific ones, such as the environment, or statistics in the news, and which are worth watching or listening to due to their topicality and fair treatment. The chapter also illustrates how visits to museums or attending talks can provide enjoyable ways to learn about STEM issues, and how technologies and methods we now take for granted have come to be. It shows how approaching organisations directly can often prove fruitful, and (finally) lists sources to help you pinpoint your own investigations.

Breaking down information

Even if you're attracted to a particular sector of STEM (say, engineering), the number of specialisms within it may still leave you confused. However, it's worth having the patience to reduce a large amount of information into bite-sized pieces. Teasing out the important features of jobs or careers whose names sound similar, but may in fact be significantly different, will let you whittle down numerous options into a few. Becoming serious about just one or two will probably take some time, but don't be discouraged – the level of commitment required later on makes your research now definitely worthwhile.

Pioneer in STEM
John Harrison (1693-1776)

John Harrison's first home was on the estate of Nostell Priory, near Wakefield, in Yorkshire, where his father was employed as a carpenter. However, before he was seven, the family moved to Lincolnshire. John became fascinated by mechanics and the laws of motion and, at 19, despite having no formal training, he built his first clock out of wood, using carpentry skills acquired from his father.

A great international problem at this time was the inability of ships' captains to know where they were on the open sea. They knew how to calculate their latitude but not their longitude. What was needed was a clock which, despite the movement of the ship, could maintain the same accuracy at sea as it did on land. Delays in arrivals and actual loss of ships rendered a solution so urgent that in the Longitude Act of 1714, Parliament offered a prize of £20,000 (equivalent to several million pounds today) to whoever first found one.

The potential reward attracted suggestions from every level of society, with more than a few being quite hare-brained. Harrison, however, threw himself into the task with boundless energy and breathtaking ingenuity. Between 1730 and 1770, he constructed five revolutionary timekeepers, now known as H1–H5 (the 'H' for 'Harrison'). Each was of increased sophistication and decreasing size, the last being little bigger than a pocket watch, yet proving accurate to within a third of a second a day when trialled at sea. King George III (a strong supporter of Harrison when not everyone was on his side) and the explorer Captain Cook were among those loudest in praise of the first chronometer.

Harrison eventually received long-overdue financial recognition of his lifetime's work and great contribution. Sadly, however, his clocks were neglected after his death and they fell into a state of disrepair. However, in the 1920s, they attracted the attention of Lieutenant Commander Robert J Gould of the Royal Navy, who, despite no formal training in horology, restored the clocks completely, a task he did without pay and which took him 12 years. Today, they are on display at the Maritime Museum at Greenwich, where they are known reverently as 'the Harrisons'.

Books, journals and websites

Books, journals and websites (including YouTube) contain large amounts of information, but it's not worth spending time on material that isn't helping you progress. No matter which publication you're reading, you can save time by starting at its contents page (rather than browsing), which should steer you towards what's most relevant. Initially, only one part may seem suitable, but reading it may make other ones appear more interesting.

Information pitched too low or too high is a turn-off for most people. It's therefore usually best to start with general careers material. Later, if you're interested, and as you learn more, you may even find out information from journals aimed at a professional readership. Make sure you visit the careers (or the main) library in your school or college first. The librarian (or even fellow students) will be able to save you time by pointing out the resources which are most useful to you. Most school or college libraries hold at least one good careers reference book and a wide range of college and university prospectuses.

Useful books and magazines

Careers (Trotman Education), published annually, with information on a huge range of jobs

Getting into Engineering Courses (Trotman Education)

For information on higher education and applications, see *HEAP: University Degree Offers*, *How to Complete Your UCAS Application Form*, *University Interviews*, *How to Write a Winning Personal Statement* and *The University Choice Journal* (all Trotman Education).

Look out, too, for good magazines written for a non-professional readership – *New Scientist* is a well-known example, and contains news of interesting developments in STEM fields. Or check out their website, www.newscientist.com.

See pages 118–119 for a list of websites for professional bodies and for help with higher education choices.

Useful websites

Here are some websites of professional bodies and publishers of careers materials in STEM-related occupational fields. They're examples of the sources which have factually accurate information presented in a (usually) unbiased way, because they're well established, don't represent any particular employer, and are in some cases not-for-profit.

Professional bodies

Biochemical Society
www.biochemistry.org

British and Irish Association of Zoos and Aquariums
www.biaza.org.uk

Chartered Institute of Ecology and Environmental Management
www.ieem.net

Chartered Society of Forensic Science
www.csofs.org

Civil Service Jobs
www.civilservice.gov.uk/jobs

Engineering Council
www.engc.org.uk

Geological Society
www.geolsoc.org.uk

Green Jobs
www.greenjobs.co.uk

Institute of Food Science and Technology
www.ifst.org

Institute of Physics
www.iop.org

Institution of Chemical Engineers
www.icheme.org

Institution of Engineering Designers
www.ied.org.uk

Marine Biological Association
www.mba.ac.uk

Institute of Mathematics
www.mathscareers.org.uk

Met Office
www.metoffice.gov.uk

National Apprenticeship Service
www.apprenticeships.org.uk

Natural Environment Research Council
www.nerc.ac.uk

Natural History Museum
www.nhm.ac.uk

NHS Careers
www.nhscareers.nhs.uk

Office for National Statistics
www.ons.gov.uk

Royal Society of Biology
www.rsb.org.uk

Royal Society of Chemistry
www.rsc.org

Royal Statistical Society
www.rss.org.uk

Science, Engineering and Manufacturing Technologies Alliance (www.semta.org.uk)

Higher education

The following resources are recommended for anyone considering to university.

Which? University
www.university.which.co.uk

The Complete University
Guide
www.thecompleteuniversity
guide.co.uk

Push Independent University
Guide
www.push.co.uk

Careers Writers' Association
website
www.parentalguidance.org.uk

General careers advice

CASCAID
www.cascaid.co.uk

Gap year
www.gap-year.com

Maths careers
www.mathscareers.org.uk

Not going to Uni
www.notgoingtouni.co.uk

Plotr
www.plotr.co.uk

TV and radio

Mainstream TV and radio offer excellent short series or one-off documentaries on developments in science and technology. Programmes like the BBC's well-respected *Panorama* often feature topics on the uses (and abuses) of science and technology, while the regular Radio 4 series *Inside Science*, *The Digital Human*, and *Costing the Earth* are all worth a listen. The series *More or Less* examines the numbers cited in news bulletins, and, by showing how statistics should be properly calculated, illustrates how often we can be misled by the ones we're given. Of course, news programmes themselves often feature stories related to science and technology, though their focus tends to be on contentious topics (such as fracking, the gas detection and retrieval method). That said, this kind of knowledge could play a part in career decision-making.

Talks and museums

Many universities offer lectures or talks on science and technology topics, sometimes as a series, or even as an evening class, lasting perhaps a term, or even an academic year. One-off presentations are normally made by a recognised expert, such as an academic researcher with a reputation in a specialist area. They can provide an excellent introduction to major STEM issues and their complexities. Entry to such events is usually free or very cheap. In addition, many museums are devoted to the history and development of science, engineering and technology. Often these reflect a once-important local industry, but some are wide-ranging. One place is the Thackray Museum in Leeds, which focuses on the development of medicine over the past two or three centuries. Another is the Industrial Museum in Bradford, whose displays include engineering since the Industrial Revolution. Visits to museums like these can remind us of how relatively recent and exciting many STEM-related developments have been. Really large collections of this kind can be seen at the Museum of Science and the Natural History Museum, both in London.

 Fascinating fact

In the early days of space flight, an American astronaut, Alan Shepard, was kept waiting in his rocket capsule while a technical problem was being fixed. Time went by, until he confessed to mission control that his bladder was getting the better of him. The experts (to his relief) declared he could pee into his pressure suit without risk. Subsequently, highly absorbent underwear was designed for all astronauts.

People and organisations

Personal contacts are an excellent way to explore STEM occupations which interest you. A family friend or neighbour already working in one might be ideal. Failing this, you might ask an appropriate teacher or college lecturer; he/she will probably know someone employed in STEM research or production, and can advise you on contacting them. Alternatively, find a suitable local organisation and ring or email; the human resources department will probably be the best place to start. Also, don't be afraid to get in touch with a university. People in the relevant department may be busy, but they'll still be polite and will help if they can – after all, people like you may be the future of their profession.

Conclusion

There are just a few last things worth saying about obtaining good careers information. It's sometimes thought that careers material must be very recent to be worth reading, but this depends on the nature of the information. Rapid advances in technology mean that STEM jobs can alter just as quickly as other occupations, but the essential activities and objectives of many, even following changes, can remain the same for a long time. Information on these central features may still be worth reading after three or four years. But details of qualification routes, entry requirements, or the job market can change from one year to the next, and you should only rely on the latest information. Try to focus on information no more than two years old.

One way in which people can assist you (but not mentioned earlier) is helping you evaluate anything you read, or are told. Parents or guardians are the obvious choice here, and may well draw your attention to something you've overlooked, or help you see the pros and cons of different options. Remember, though, that they're unlikely to be careers experts, so also check with your careers adviser or a member of school/college staff.

Lastly, see who's produced any information you use. Most careers material is written by organisations not intending to influence your decisions. However, any from ones who seem keen to sign you up should be treated cautiously. If what they're offering sounds too good to be true, make sure you have a few questions ready to ask if you approach them. Hopefully things will really be as good as they sound!

STEM Careers A-Z

List of careers featured in this section:

Accountant
Acoustician
Actuary
Aeronautical engineer
Aerospace engineer
   ing technician
Agricultural engineer
Analytical scientist
Archaeologist
Architect
Astronomer
Auditor
Automobile engineer
Biochemist
Broadcast engineer
Chemical engineer
Colour technologist
Computer games
   programmer
Computer games
   tester
Control engineer
Dental technician
Dentist
Doctor
E-Learning designer
Ecologist

Electronic/electrical
   engineer
Engineering
   draughtsperson
Financial adviser
Food quality analyst
Forensic scientist
Gas network
   engineer
Geologist
Geophysicist
Horologist
Hydrologist
Industrial chemist
Information security
   analyst
IT service manager
IT systems
   programmer
Laboratory technician
Map-maker
Marine biologist
Maths teacher
Metallurgist
Meteorologist
Nanotechnologist
Nuclear engineer

Nurse
Nutritionist
Oceanographer
Offshore engineer
Orthotist
Palaeontologist
Pharmacist
Physicist
Physiotherapist
Plumber
Quantity surveyor
Radiographer
Science teacher
Soil scientist
Speech and language
   therapist
Statistician
Surveyor
Telecommunications
   engineer
Theatre sound
   technician
Vehicle technician
Virologist
Website designer
Welder
Zoological scientist

On the following pages are, in alphabetical order, 70 jobs chosen to represent STEM occupations. In a book of this size, they can't aim to be comprehensive. Rather, they're intended to illustrate how broad the range is, while hinting at how specialised it's possible to become. They include a selection from each of the four subdivisions – science (S), technology (T), engineering (E) and maths (M). However, these are not equally represented with, for instance, clearly fewer maths jobs than science ones. This is because the letter in brackets after the occupation only shows the subdivision it most reflects; for instance, a job marked (E) for engineering might still require considerable mathematical aptitude. The letters are therefore included only in an effort to convey each job's *essential* character.

Accountant (M)

Accountants work for organisations or individuals to ensure their finances conform to regulations, and provide them with a good rate of monetary return. They examine not only how money has been spent or invested, but how it might be in the future. The profession has three major fields of operations – the public sector, industry and commerce, and public practice. (See also page 19.)

 ## Acoustician (S)

Acousticians use their knowledge of the physics of sound to better manage it. This involves improving sound quality, reducing noise levels and helping organisations to find the causes of unwanted noise, and solutions to it.

 ## Actuary (M)

Actuaries calculate the likelihood of future events to enable organisations to estimate the risk levels essential to setting insurance premiums. They need a strong mathematical aptitude to understand and apply theories of probability, and make sophisticated use of statistics. (See also page 33.)

 ## Aeronautical engineer (E)

Aeronautical engineers use scientific principles and a deep knowledge of aerodynamics and mechanical engineering to design, construct and maintain aircraft. The majority work on planes, but some on radar, missiles, satellites, or even space vehicles. (See also page 14.)

 ## Aerospace engineering technician (E)

Aerospace engineering technicians are mostly involved in building and testing aircraft, and repairing and servicing them between flights. They use sophisticated equipment to detect wear and tear and may specialise, normally in small planes, large passenger jets, or helicopters.

 ## Agricultural engineer (E)

Agricultural engineers design, develop, test and manage equipment used in farming, horticulture, and forestry, and in maintaining recreational surfaces such as sports fields and golf courses. Much of the machinery they make is used to cultivate soil, harvest crops, store land produce, or feed livestock.

Analytical scientist (S)

Analytical scientists normally work in laboratories, establishing the exact nature of substances brought or delivered to them, usually by organisations. Their work is very broad ranging, but helps protect the environment, ensure standards of food, drink and drugs, diagnose disease and guarantee the safety of manufacturing processes.

 ## Archaeologist (S)

Archaeologists study the human past, initially through physical remains, such as bones, pottery, tools and (sometimes) buildings. Excavating remains must be done with great care, to preserve them in the best possible state for examination and analysis, often using sophisticated equipment and techniques. Many archaeologists are employed by museum services, universities or large organisations devoted to preserving the past, such as English Heritage.

 ## Architect (E)

Architects plan and design buildings and are involved in their construction until completed. Their commission may be for a single structure (like a school, library or community centre) or many similar ones (such as a housing estate) or to renovate one, possibly a listed building. (See also page 10.)

 ## Astronomer (S)

Most astronomers work at a university or observatory studying the stars and planets, and other celestial phenomena. Typically they use equipment such as telescopes and satellites to collect data (called 'observational' work) or employ computer models to test ideas of what happens in space (known as 'theoretical' work). (See also page 7.)

 ## Auditor (M)

Auditors are specialist independent accountants, who check that the financial records of organisations in both the public and private sectors meet legal requirements. They gather the information through computer and paper records, and also by talking to staff employed by the organisation they're inspecting. This helps provide enough understanding to reach a fair judgment of its financial activities. The audit report they produce goes to the organisation's board of directors.

Automobile engineer (E)

Automobile engineers are often employed by car manufacturers, but also have a lot of work developing public transport vehicles, emergency service ones, or even competitive sports cars. Those specialising in research and development may seek to improve passenger safety, while others try to reduce carbon emissions or to maximise fuel efficiency. (See also page 17.)

 ## Biochemist (S)

Biochemists study life processes at molecular level in all manner of organisms, from visible ones (such as plants and animals) to those seen only under a microscope. They may work in industry, helping develop new, safe foods; in agriculture, improving fertilisers or pesticides; or in medicine, analysing body tissues and fluids to aid in diagnosing disease.

 ## Broadcast engineer (T)

Broadcast engineers use and develop the equipment which makes the transmission of TV and radio programmes possible. Those specialising in outside broadcasts may find themselves working anywhere in the country, or even the world, while those doing research and development are normally studio-based, often replacing traditional services with increasingly popular digital text ones.

 ## Chemical engineer (S)

Chemical engineers are knowledgeable about the processes which cause changes in the composition of substances. Their expertise is essential to converting raw materials into complex products such as fibres, plastics, paints, drugs, dyes and cleaning agents. (See also page 30.)

 ## Colour technologist (T)

Colour technologists research and develop dyes and pigments (collectively known as colorants), or are involved in the actual process of colouring the materials themselves, which include paper, textiles, fibres, food products, detergents and soap.

Computer games programmer (T)

Computer games programmers convert the specifications of designers into games appropriate for a range of devices, such as console, tablet, or mobile phone, either by writing computer code themselves, or employing equipment which does this. Most current games are very complex, so a programmer normally performs as one of a team.

 ## Computer games tester (T)

Computer games testers play these games to ensure they work properly, often doing this for different levels or versions of the product. They record any problems or 'bugs' they find, and may also check that what's said in instructions and on packaging is correct, compare the game with similar ones on the market, and recommend possible improvements.

 ## Control engineer (E)

Control engineers research, design and manage the equipment which guides and monitors machinery, usually in the form of electronic or computer technology. They need to understand the nature and limits of human capacity, as well as how machines operate. (See also page 29.)

 ## Dental technician (T)

Working to the instructions of a dentist or doctor, dental technicians make and repair dental appliances, the majority being crowns, bridges and dentures. Great precision is important, and they use a wide range of materials, including metal alloys, plastics and ceramics. (See also page 27.)

 ## Dentist (S)

Dentists mostly see patients for regular check-ups to prevent tooth decay or gum disease. Treatments include scaling and polishing teeth, drilling and filling cavities, and extractions. Dentists also straighten irregular teeth, and fit crowns, bridges or dentures. They are assisted by dental nurses, and may also supervise dental hygienists or therapists. Most dentists work in high-street practices, but some are hospital-based, where they are usually employed to offer a specialism.

Doctor (S)

Doctors diagnose and treat ill health, and (where possible) act to prevent its occurrence. Most are either GPs or hospital doctors, the latter including numerous specialisms. Most doctors need excellent communication skills because they need to offer information and advice to patients. Most also belong to a team, which may include nurses, radiographers, pharmacists or dieticians. Some doctors become researchers and may have little or no contact with patients.

 ## E-Learning designer (T)

E-learning designers produce software for educational and training purposes, often for users without an instructor. The facilities they present must therefore communicate fully and precisely, as well as attractively and interestingly. Besides technical knowledge, they need to understand how people learn, or work with a specialist who does.

 ## Ecologist (S)

Ecologists study the relationships between plants, animals, people and the space they inhabit, to contribute to environmental protection, both through action and advice. They help restore areas which have been spoiled or contaminated, monitor wildlife and manage areas set aside for conservation. (See also page 24.)

 ## Electronic/electrical engineer (E)

Electronic engineers research and design telecommunications systems, computers, satellite systems and television, while electrical engineers ensure the generation and supply of electricity for domestic, commercial and industrial purposes. Some act as consultants, and may train their customers to use new systems properly.

 ## Engineering draughtsperson (E)

There are two stages in the engineering drawing process – 'design' and 'detail'. The first involves making a scale drawing showing the general outline, along with details of the nature and number of parts required, while the second consists of producing the very precise drawings which the production-line staff refer to at each stage of the manufacturing process.

Financial adviser (M)

Financial advisers constructively encourage their clients to make good decisions about many related products such as savings, pensions, life insurance and mortgages. They are independent, so not restricted to advising on the products of a sole organisation, such as a bank or building society. Once the client has reached a decision, or expressed a preference, the adviser makes the necessary arrangements, such as setting up an investment. Advisers must keep up to date with the state of financial markets and the new products which are constantly being designed. Many advisers provide their clients with a comprehensive plan to cover current needs and look at likely future ones, such as for retirement, or paying for a child's education.

 ## Food quality analyst (T)

Food quality analysts (or food technicians) are usually laboratory-based, where they help develop food products and test them for quality and safety. As well as food features such as taste and colour, they check raw ingredients and storage methods to safeguard against dangerous micro-organisms like salmonella and E. coli. (See also page 23.)

 ## Forensic scientist (S)

Forensic scientists provide scientific evidence (much of it very small, physically) for use in courts of law. They may work within a police force, but do so as civilian employees, and must approach their tasks impartially. These are mostly done in a laboratory environment, but are sometimes at the scene of a crime. As well as providing evidence in a written report, they may be quizzed on it in court.

 ## Gas network engineer (E)

Usually working as part of a team, gas network engineers install gas supply to houses, industrial and commercial premises, schools and hospitals, and other public buildings. Having installed it, they ensure the safe continuance of the supply and provide an emergency service as needed.

 ## Geologist (S)

Geologists study rocks, minerals, fossils, crystals and sediments to learn more about our planet and its resources. The potential applications of their knowledge include oil and gas exploration, mining, geological surveying and civil engineering. (See also page 26.)

Geophysicist (S)

Geophysicists study the physical make-up, motion and other workings of the earth. Their activities often result in very precise mapping of specific features or areas, which can be essential in locating and extracting mineral resources, or those vital to life itself, like water. Sometimes they can act as specialists within another occupation, like archaeology.

 ## Horologist (T)

Horologists repair and restore watches and clocks, most specialising in one or the other. This entails dismantling and cleaning the mechanism, and repairing or replacing damaged or worn parts. They use small tools, including eyeglasses and tweezers, to operate very precisely. Some watch repairers specialise in mechanical items, some in quartz, some in electronic. Clock repairers may specialise in domestic or public ones, some in antique ones, which usually means working in their owners' homes.

 ## Hydrologist (S)

Hydrologists monitor and manage water resources in a range of settings and used for different purposes, some domestic, others industrial, commercial or environmental. They ensure an effective flow of water through pipes or channels, and contribute to effective planning and sustainability of water resources, including their cost-effectiveness.

 ## Industrial chemist (S)

Industrial chemists involved in research and development try to arrive at materials with characteristics vital or desirable in a new product. Those involved in the production process must ensure large quantities of the material can be turned out within budget, and that the production staff who undertake this are properly trained. (See also page 10.)

 ## Information security analyst (T)

Information security analysts plan and implement measures designed to shield an organisation's computer networks from cyber-attacks. This entails scrutinising existing systems and making changes where necessary to offset weaknesses. They write instructions to help the organisation in the event of a breach, and may be involved in related staff training.

IT service manager (T)

IT service managers co-ordinate advice and support to customers during and after sales of computer systems, much of this being delivered through a help desk team which they head. They may visit potential customers to demonstrate systems, and advise on possible additional facilities, before drawing up a service level agreement. Most service managers liaise with suppliers, and may also train staff.

 ## IT systems programmer (T)

IT systems programmers research, design and write programs for controlling the workings of mainframe computers and computer networks. They may also install and support these, which include monitoring data storage, information transmission and the device's links with other systems in general, while maximising security at all times.

 ## Laboratory technician (T)

Laboratory technicians are employed in a wide range of areas, including industry, education, research, medicine and commerce. Most help professionals engaged in biology-related work, and their regular duties normally include setting up equipment, preparing and carrying out experiments, taking measurements and writing reports or summaries, as well as disposing of waste and ordering fresh stocks.

 ## Map-maker (M)

Map-makers (also known as cartographers) prepare maps and sea charts, globes of the earth's surface, three-dimensional models of geographical areas, and even representations of the night sky. Besides existing maps, they also use aerial photographs or seismic sensing to produce finished graphics, whose nature will depend largely on whether they're intended for non-experts or professionals. (See also page 31.)

 ## Marine biologist (S)

Marine biologists study sea creatures and the environment on which they depend, to raise our understanding of the marine world and to predict changes in ecosystems which may prove significant. They mostly work close to the coast or on the open sea and contribute to conservation, education and research. A project could take them anywhere in the world. (See also page 8.)

Maths teacher (M)

Teachers can operate as maths specialists from the beginning of secondary level (Year 7 or equivalent). Maths is a compulsory subject up to and including GCSE (or equivalent), so most of them teach to all levels of ability. The main areas taught are called number (arithmetic), algebra, geometry, probability and statistics. (See also page 18.)

 ## Metallurgist (S)

Metallurgists use their knowledge of metals and alloys (including iron, steel, nickel and aluminium) to design a wide range of products, and ensure their safe performance. Civil engineering and the aeronautical and motor industries are among those which could not function without them. (See also page 29.)

 ## Meteorologist (S)

Meteorologists study the sciences of weather and climate to make short- and long-term forecasts. They do this by collecting and interpreting abundant data relating to atmospheric pressure, temperature, humidity, wind and clouds in order to build computer models geared to this. A few become well known as weather presenters on TV. (See also page 31.)

 ## Nanotechnologist (T)

Nanotechnologists design and build devices on a tiny scale. They normally work in a laboratory, wearing protective clothing, and using specialist scientific equipment. They're mainly employed in industries such as electronics, energy production and storage, automotive, aerospace, biotechnology, medicine and pharmaceuticals, and food science and production.

 ## Nuclear engineer (E)

Nuclear engineers design nuclear plants, supervise the manufacture of the equipment used there, and operate the finished installations. They must guarantee a safe environment in the installation and surrounding area, and shut down the plant when required for maintenance or inspection, or in an emergency. They retrieve, treat and store radioactive waste from the site, and develop waste management strategies, which have to be for the very long term.

 **Nurse (S)**

Nurses work in one of four specialist branches – adult nursing, mental health, learning disability and children's nursing – and look after people who are unwell, or who need special care, sometimes long term. They do practical tasks like dressing wounds or administering drugs, but also plan how to meet their patients' needs. Many work in hospitals, but also increasingly in GP surgeries and community clinics. Within the four main branches, there are specialisms such as intensive care, cancer care and theatre nursing, each of which can require a particular aptitude or disposition.

 Nutritionist (S)

Nutritionists are knowledgeable in the science of how our bodies use food, and the way this relates to good health and illness. They advise people on eating healthily in order to avoid serious conditions such as heart disease, cancer, stroke or diabetes. Many work in the NHS or the food industry (in research or labelling), but they can also be employed in the community, co-ordinating healthier eating programmes in schools, teaching cooking skills or communicating health information online. In some settings, they must work under a GP or a dietician. Some work for charities or within sports, as a personal trainer, or part of a competitive professional team.

 Oceanographer (S)

Oceanographers study the earth's oceans and seas and how these interact with the atmosphere and land masses. Most of their data are collected on the water, using research vessels, instruments or floats, or robotic devices. They use this knowledge to promote responsible use of marine resources and to minimise environmental damage.

 Offshore engineer (E)

Offshore engineers design, construct and operate offshore rigs used in drilling beneath the seabed for oil and gas. They are constantly aiming to accomplish this faster and more accurately and computer-aided design (CAD) helps them achieve this.

 Orthotist (T)

Orthotists design and fit surgical devices (such as spine supports, neck collars, and callipers) to support part of a patient's body, usually to relieve pain or act for atrophied or paralysed muscles. They also make any adjustments, repairs or renewals as the need arises. (See also page 26.)

Palaeontologist (S)

Palaeontologists study fossils to build their knowledge of life forms which existed in the very distant past. The clues these provide about this past offer important data concerning environmental and climate change.

 Pharmacist (S)

Pharmacists are very knowledgeable about medicines and drugs and their actual or potential effects on the human body, including allergic reactions. They may work in the community (normally in retail premises or a medical centre) or in hospitals, ensuring people receive the right products and in the correct dosages. Some work in industry, where they research, develop and test new medicines.

 Physicist (S)

Physicists study a wide range of phenomena to better understand how the earth, and even the universe, work. Their findings contribute significantly to the development and improvement of countless products and services, especially within areas like IT, engineering, instrumentation, meteorology and transport.

 Physiotherapist (S)

Physiotherapists assess and treat people with restricted movement, typically caused by age, illness, or injury. Most of the problems they address relate to joints or bones, but some to the cardiovascular (heart and lung) and nervous systems. They work in hospitals and outpatient clinics, workplaces (possibly in connection with industrial accidents), in older people's homes (following a stroke, perhaps) and advising women on exercise and posture in antenatal and postnatal care. GPs and other healthcare professionals often refer patients to physiotherapists. Some work in specialist areas where treatment has to go hand in hand with lifestyle change (e.g. giving up smoking).

 Plumber (T)

Plumbers install, maintain and repair hot and cold water systems, central heating and drainage, and the pipes and controls used for gas supply. They may work in houses, and commercial or industrial premises, often needing to consult complex plans or drawings before taking action. They need considerable skill to properly use a wide variety of tools to cut, bend and join metals and plastics.

Quantity surveyor (M)

Quantity surveyors calculate the cost of building projects, taking account of materials, labour and maintenance. Many work for commercial contractors, and are based on a site, usually for housing. However, some are employed by local authorities, where they're more likely to engage in single-structure programmes, whether new or for renovation.

 ## Radiographer (T)

Radiographers work in either diagnostics or therapeutics. The former produce precise images of the body which aid diagnosis of conditions, monitor the progress of a condition, or a patient's rate of a recovery. They have long used X-rays, but more recently introduced facilities include magnetic resonance imaging (MRI), ultrasound and computed tomography to build up two- and three-dimensional images. Therapeutic radiographers work as part of a team treating cancer patients, operating with great precision to deliver exact doses of radiation to affected body areas.

 ## Science teacher (S)

Most specialist science teachers work in secondary schools, covering one or more of biology, chemistry, physics and geology. Like English and maths, science is compulsory to GCSE, and many students take one or more from this group to A level (or equivalent). Skill is needed in using science equipment, and some projects may require fieldwork. Health and safety considerations are always a priority.

 ## Soil scientist (S)

Soils are vital for producing food, timber and fibres, as well as sustaining ecological habitats and encouraging biodiversity. Soil scientists collect and analyse soil samples to guarantee appropriate selection and encourage proper usage, as well as ensuring they don't become exhausted owing to excessive cultivation.

 ## Speech and language therapist (S)

Speech and language therapists work mainly with children and adults who have problems in producing or understanding speech, suffer from a stammer or have difficulty swallowing. These often result from hearing loss, stroke, disability, injury or a degenerative condition. Therapists must quickly establish a trusting relationship with each client to make an accurate diagnosis leading to effective treatment. Their work is mainly with individuals but may include group sessions. Therapists often consult doctors, nurses and psychologists, and may work in schools and day-care centres, as well as hospitals, surgeries and clients' own homes.

 ### Statistician (M)

Statisticians collect, analyse and interpret numerical data. They must act neutrally, presenting actual findings arrived at by respected methods, never being swayed by what they (or those who employ them) might prefer the results to be. Many work for the Civil Service or in local government. (See also page 20.)

 ### Surveyor (M)

While some surveyors are employed in specialist fields, most work in land or property, taking measurements and making estimates of value. Many are involved in house sales, where they check properties for structural damage or instability, and draw attention to any hazards or shortcomings in functions. (See also page 12.)

 ### Telecommunications engineer (T)

Telecommunications engineers try to improve existing communications technology, and to develop new products. The focus of their work is on areas like mobile phones, and cable and satellite systems, and in co-ordinating telephone and computer systems. They can set up video conferencing links too. (See also page 16.)

 ### Theatre sound technician (T)

Theatre sound technicians set up and operate sound equipment for live productions such as plays and musicals. They must maintain this apparatus, which in a touring production may need to be dismantled after each show. Setting up equipment to produce good-quality sound requires considerable expertise, as every theatre is different. (See also page 28.)

Vehicle technician (T)

Vehicle technicians service, overhaul and repair light vehicles (such as cars and motorcycles) or heavy ones (such as buses or trucks). They're very skilled at diagnosing faults and often work under pressure to quickly repair vehicles needed promptly. Some technicians specialise in construction plant, such as diggers or cranes.

 ### Virologist (S)

Virologists study viral infections like hepatitis and HIV. Many work within a clinical microbiology service, identifying and noting the nature of viruses which cause infection. They may screen selected populations at risk from specific viral diseases, and sometimes investigate the spread of infections by scrutinising the design and maintenance of clinical areas (like operating theatres), food preparation and hygiene, or cleaning and waste disposal procedures.

 ### Website designer (T)

Website designers (sometimes also called developers) use computer knowledge and design skills to produce pages featured on internet websites. A well-produced site combines a pleasing appearance with easy-to-navigate information. Some designers may enjoy considerable creative freedom, while others may have to conform to an organisation's company style.

 ### Welder (E)

Welders use intense heat to join together pieces of metal, often operating in a workshop or on a construction site. Normally they use an electric arc or a gas flame, and wear considerable protective clothing, including a helmet, thick gloves and boots, and (often) ear protectors. In some industries, like car manufacture, most of the operations are done by robots, but welders set up and guide the machines themselves.

 ### Zoological scientist (S)

Zoological scientists study animals in the wild and in captivity to help them live contentedly, and ensure their long-term survival. Many are attached to zoos, safari parks, or universities, though project work often takes them abroad, sometimes to remote and exotic places. Technological developments have now made minute and continuous observation of animal behaviour much easier and less obtrusive.

Index of advertisers

EngineeringUK — colour plate section
Institute of Physics — colour plate section
Oxford Brookes University — 38–39, colour plate section
Royal Aeronautical Society — 15, colour plate section
Royal Society of Chemistry — colour plate section
University of York — 65, colour plate section